Learner-Centered Design of Computing Education

Research on Computing for Everyone

Synthesis Lectures on Human-Centered Informatics

Editor
John M. Carroll, *Penn State University*

Human-Centered Informatics (HCI) is the intersection of the cultural, the social, the cognitive, and the aesthetic with computing and information technology. It encompasses a huge range of issues, theories, technologies, designs, tools, environments and human experiences in knowledge, work, recreation and leisure activity, teaching and learning, and the potpourri of everyday life. The series publishes state-of-the-art syntheses, case studies, and tutorials in key areas. It shares the focus of leading international conferences in HCI.

Learner-Centered Design of Computing Education: Research on Computing for Everyone
Mark Guzdial
2015

The Envisionment and Discovery Collaboratory (EDC): Explorations in Human-Centered Informatics
Ernesto G. Arias, Hal Eden, and Gerhard Fischer
2015

Humanistic HCI
Jeffrey Bardzell and Shaowen Bardzell
2015

The Paradigm Shift to Multimodality in Contemporary Computer Interfaces
Sharon Oviatt and Philip R. Cohen
2015

Multitasking in the Digital Age
Gloria Mark
2015

The Design of Implicit Interactions
Wendy Ju
2015

Learner-Centered Design of Computing Education: Research on Computing for Everyone

Mark Guzdia

ISBN: 978-3-031-01088-0   paperback
ISBN: 978-3-031-02216-6   ebook

DOI 10.1007/978-3-031-02216-6

A Publication in the Springer series
SYNTHESIS LECTURES ON HUMAN-CENTERED INFORMATICS

Lecture #33
Series Editor: John M. Carroll, *Penn State University*
Series ISSN
Print 1946-7680   Electronic 1946-7699

Learner-Centered Design of Computing Education

Research on Computing for Everyone

Mark Guzdial

School of Interactive Computing, College of Computing
Georgia Institute of Technology

SYNTHESIS LECTURES ON HUMAN-CENTERED INFORMATICS #33

ABSTRACT

Computing education is in enormous demand. Many students (both children and adult) are realizing that they will need programming in the future. This book presents the argument that they are not all going to use programming in the same way and for the same purposes. What do we mean when we talk about teaching *everyone* to program? When we target a broad audience, should we have the same goals as computer science education for professional software developers? *How* do we design computing education that works for everyone? This book proposes use of a *learner-centered design* approach to create computing education for a broad audience. It considers several reasons for teaching computing to everyone and how the different reasons lead to different choices about learning goals and teaching methods. The book reviews the history of the idea that programming isn't just for the professional software developer. It uses research studies on teaching computing in liberal arts programs, to graphic designers, to high school teachers, in order to explore the idea that computer science for everyone requires us to re-think how we teach and what we teach. The conclusion describes how we might create computing education for everyone.

KEYWORDS

computer science education, computing education, learner-centered design

Dedicated to Elliot, Janet, Jim,
Peter, Rich, John, Alan, and all my mentors.

Contents

Preface

Some of the earliest work in computing education is about the value of computing and programming *for everyone*, or at least not just for professional programmers. The pioneers of this perspective included Alan Perlis, Seymour Papert, Alan Kay, Adele Goldberg, Cynthia Solomon, and Andrea diSessa. When those early computer scientists started talking about the value of computing for learning, there was no enormous demand for a programming labor force. Instead, they argued that computing was an important medium for learning. Today, computing has become so important for our modern society, and the need for programming labor is so great that the power of computing as a medium for expression and thought may no longer be considered.

My personal introduction to this perspective was when I first read *Personal Dynamic Media* [169] over 30 years ago, and the vision continues to inspire me. Now, I realize that there is a wide range of desired learning outcomes from computing education.

Unfortunately, most of a computer science education today is about getting better at producing software developers. The goal is greater productivity of higher-quality software developers. The annual SIGCSE Technical Symposium is mostly a meeting of over 1000 undergraduate computer science teachers, where their shared goal is to provide great teaching to contribute workers to the software industry. I share that goal, but I believe that there is a broader picture of providing access to the advantages of computing as a tool to think with to everyone who wants it.

This book is a review of the research literature on teaching computing to everyone. My goal is to be most useful to new researchers who want to understand the narrative of teaching programming to students, from the 1960's to today. Teachers may find this book useful to see different perspectives on how to design computing education for different purposes. While this book addresses the use of different teaching methods for different audiences, my goal is not to offer teaching methods. The best book I know for how to become a computer science teacher is the 2011 *Guide to Teaching Computer Science* [234]. This book focuses on understanding learners and their issues and on supporting learning by students who *are* and also others who *aren't* aiming to be professional software developers. Call this latter category "computing education *for the rest of us*."

Mark Guzdial
November 2015

Acknowledgments

The idea for this book came out of discussions with Josh Tenenberg and Jane Margolis. Josh and I talked about helping new researchers to connect computing education to other research in education and learning sciences. I hope that this book helps with making those connections. When Jane was working on *Stuck in the Shallow End* [203], she told me that she wished that there was already a book that talked about the kinds of computer science that could be taught more broadly, that argued for the importance of everyone learning about computing. Since then, Yasmin Kafai and Quinn Burke wrote *Connected Code: Why Children Need to Learn Programming* [160] which makes that argument for children better than I could. This book aims to continue that story to explore why we might want *everyone* to learn programming, from children through undergraduates and to adults, and how we might achieve that goal.

My thanks to the many colleagues who worked on the research that I describe in this book. I offer my apologies in advance for where I got it wrong.

My great thanks to those who read early drafts of this book. Peter Denning was the first of my readers, and he gave me valuable insights for which I'm grateful. Greg Wilson and Nick Falkner did an amazing job of wading through the whole document and helping me see where my words did not mean what I meant them to mean. Mike Hewner, Lijun Ni, and Lana Yarosh kindly reviewed the book to make sure that what I said about them were true (to the best of their recollection). My students at Georgia Tech were also helpful in spotting errors when we used a draft of this book in a seminar. You can be sure that mistakes and erroneous conclusions in this volume are my fault for not listening better to my readers.

I am grateful also to those reviewers who read the draft that I submitted to Diane Cerra at Morgan & Claypool. Quintin Cutts, Sally Fincher, Kathi Fisler, Alan Kay, Mike McCracken, Scott McCrickard, Chris Quintana, Mary Beth Rosson, and Elliot Soloway put in an enormous amount of time reading the whole thing, pointing out questions, and helping me understand how much a gap there was between the submitted draft and a useful book. The book is much closer to useful due to their attention and efforts, for which I thank them all.

The work at Georgia Tech was supported by several *National Science Foundation* grants, including NSF grants CNS-0512213, CNS-0618674, CNS-0634629, and CNS-0940394. Any opinions, findings, and conclusions or recommendations expressed in this material are those of the authors and do not necessarily reflect the views of the National Science Foundation.

I have dedicated the book to my mentors who have helped a learning scientist with an education degree succeed in a computing world, especially Elliot Soloway, Janet Kolodner, Jim Foley, Peter Freeman, Rich LeBlanc, John Stasko, and Alan Kay. I have been fortunate in having many mentors and advisors. When I graduated with my Ph.D. and received my offer to join Georgia

Tech, Elliot and I met and talked through strategy. Was there any way that a computing education guy could get tenured in a College of Computing? Thanks to my mentors, I have been able to succeed in a research-focused computer science department in the U.S. while doing computing education research. I needed all of their help to still be here.

Finally, my thanks to my wife, Barbara Ericson. She supported me during my Logo and Emile days, and has been my research partner for over a dozen years now. I am grateful for her support in all the crazy projects I take on, like this book.

Mark Guzdial
November 2015

CHAPTER 1

What Does Computing for Everyone Mean?

Over the last year, three large U.S. school districts and an entire state announced plans to offer computer science education to all children in all of their schools. Chicago [45], San Francisco [43], and then in September 2015, the largest school system in the United States, New York City [308], announced multi-year plans to make computer science education ubiquitous—every grade in every school would have some computer science learning activities. An entire state, Arkansas [174], has made a similar pledge. Parents and teachers want their kids to know about computing [83]. The President of the United States took an "Hour to Code" (in December 2014) to become the first sitting president to write a line of programming code [214]. This is an international phenomenon as in the last five years the United Kingdom [30], New Zealand [17, 18], and Denmark [42] (among others) have begun national computing curricula. There is a sense that knowledge about computer science is important, and important enough that everyone needs to have it.

As teachers and designers of education, the first question we should ask is, "Why?" Why is learning about computer science so important? Answering that question helps us to answer: "What do we want students to know or be able to do?" Once we do that, we can determine what should be taught, to whom, and how.

This book reviews the research on teaching computing to everyone. Alan Perlis first suggested that we teach computer science to everyone on a university campus in 1961 [115]. From then until now, many have explored this idea, for a wide variety of purposes. Researchers and visionaries like Seymour Papert [238], Cynthia Solomon [292], Alan Kay [169], and Andrea diSessa [65] saw the computer as a new medium for human expression and empowerment. Today, most of the arguments that I read for computing in schools are based on jobs.

The purpose of this book is to point out that there is more than one possible learning outcome from teaching computing to a broad range of people. Different people have different learning goals. There is more than one kind of computing education.

1.1 DEFINING TERMS: COMPUTING EDUCATION, COMPUTER SCIENCE, AND PROGRAMMING

In this book, I will primarily use the term *computing education*, rather than *computer science education*. I belong to the College of Computing at Georgia Tech. We're a College of *Computing* rather than *Computer Science* because the term "computing" was introduced in the reports from an influential task force led by Peter Denning, *Computing as a Discipline* [55, 58]. Computing is defined to be broader than computer science. Computing is driven by connecting computer science to other disciplines. It includes fields like information science and studies, information technology, software engineering, and computer engineering. Computer science, and computing more broadly, is about more than programming.

Computer science education is learning about computer science. The term computer science is narrower than computing. It describes well the core of computing. The computer science that we might teach in elementary and primary school would be useful and common across computing disciplines like information science, information technology, and others.

Computing education research is concerned with how people come to understand computing and how to facilitate that understanding. To understand computing means to have a robust mental model of the computer—what it can do and what it cannot do. A student with a robust mental model of the computer should be able to predict what the computer will do for a given list of instructions, a *program* [125]. Benedict duBoulay defined the term *notional machine*, that is, a mental model of what a computer can do and how to control it [78]. Any advanced use of computing, including information system design, cybersecurity risk assessment, and scientific computation, requires the practitioner to think in terms of what is possible on a computer and what is not, based on the computer's limitations—that's the notional machine.

Programming (or sometimes *coding*) is the process of writing programs. Programs do not have to be text. A variety of notations can instruct a computer to behave in a certain way. That behavior is a *process*. A program specifies a computational process which can be executed at some time in the future.

A programmer needs an accurate and robust notional machine and facility with defining the list of instructions for the computer to achieve desired ends. Programming is not the only reason to have a robust mental model of the computer. If we want people to be able to use the computer expressively, they need to know the computer's capabilities and limitations. The ability to use the computer to express ideas and to consume others' ideas is known as *computational literacy*.

Expression in this sense does not only mean creative expression. Einstein's famous equation $E = mc^2$ expresses a complex idea, and the notation allows us to think about the concepts being represented in many ways. We know that if we convert more mass to energy, we will get more energy than if we converted less. Algebraic equations are not good for expressing causality and time. Programs are better for expressing those ideas, as is discussed further in Chapter 3.

The role of programming in achieving computational literacy is an important research question. Can we develop a robust mental model of a computer *without* programming? Does computational literacy include programming? Can I develop a notional machine without writing and testing programs?

My prediction is that the answer is that programming is necessary to develop computational literacy. What we know about learning suggests that we gain new concepts first *declaratively*.

We read about the new concepts. We write about them. We talk about them. That process is facilitated by having a notation. Imagine trying to learn the concepts of *number* and *arithmetic* without having symbols like 2 and + and 3. Language existed before it was in a written form, but literature and literacy did not.

A robust notional machine is complex. It has lots of concepts embedded in it, some of which I will describe over the next few chapters. Learning a notional machine without any kind of notation is like teaching poetry only through memorized and spoken words. It may be possible, at least for simple bits of poetry. However, it's a lot easier and you can explore more powerful ideas if you can read it.

To a great extent, understanding how people come to learn programming is the critical challenge of computing education research. The challenges we face in helping a student learn the concepts in computing appear also in the challenges of teaching programming. Raymond Lister suggests that reading programs is a necessary developmental stage to writing programs and being able to predict the computer's behavior for a given program [196, 309]. It seems likely that developing a notional machine requires the ability to both read and write programs.

1.2 WHY SHOULD EVERYONE LEARN COMPUTING?

The various efforts to teach computing to everyone have had different reasons. If we know the desired end state, we can consider what is a reasonable set of learning goals and methods for achieving those goals. Similarly, we can decide when a set of goals and methods do not help us to achieve the desired end state.

1.2.1 JOBS

The day after Mayor de Blasio made the announcement of New York City's bold plan to teach computing to everyone, an open letter was released signed by over two dozen technology industry representatives, including the President of Microsoft, the CIO of Google, and a co-founder of Facebook. They praised the announcement and wrote:

> We need talent, we need it now, and we simply cannot find enough.

One argument to teach everyone about computing is that we need more workers who can program. The hope is that we can get more people to become programmers by introducing programming in school. The United States Bureau of Labor Statistics estimates that software development is one of the fastest growing job categories [35], and a high percentage of jobs in the future (over 50% of all STEM-related[1] jobs) will require knowledge of computer science [85]. Our research evidence shows that some computer science in school (even as late as high school or as an undergraduate) can be effective for developing a motivation to pursue a career in computing [134].

---

[1]STEM is an acronym for Science, Technology, Engineering, and Mathematics.

If the focus is on jobs, then the *authenticity* of the computing education becomes important [281]. We would expect the content of the course to be related to what computing professionals do. We would expect the assessment of the course to be measuring what's relevant to a computing professional.

1.2.2   LEARN ABOUT THEIR WORLD

The Computing at School working group in the UK had a slightly different goal. They want their students to learn about computing because it is part of *foundational principles and ideas* [157]. Computing is part of students' lives. We ask students to study chemistry because they live in a world where there are chemical interactions. We ask students to study biology because they live a living world. They also live in a computational world, and the reality of computation is probably going to impact their daily lives more than remembering the structure of a benzene ring or the stages of mitosis.

1.2.3   COMPUTATIONAL THINKING

Jeannette Wing coined the term *computational thinking* in 2006 when she directed computing research at the United States National Science Foundation (NSF). She wrote an influential article in the *Communications of the ACM* [326], where she argued that the way computer scientists think about the world is useful in other contexts.

> Computational thinking involves solving problems, designing systems, and under-standing human behavior, by drawing on the concepts fundamental to computer science. Computational thinking includes a range of mental tools that reflect the breadth of the field of computer science.

Her definition was related to the *algorithmic thinking* described by Newell, Perlis, and Simon in 1967 [224], but she went beyond defining what computer scientists did. She was not defining the core of computer science (as Denning did [57]). Rather, she was describing what computer science as a field offered to laypeople. In 2010, she offered a concise definition of computational thinking [325]:

> Computational thinking is the thought processes involved in formulating problems and their solutions so that the solutions are represented in a form that can effectively be carried out by an information-processing agent.

Wing's examples of computational thinking make two kinds of claims about what might be gained from learning about computing.

- The first set is about *applying computing ideas to facilitate computing work in other disciplines*. She talks about the power of computing to enhance statistics to scale much larger problems and to provide data-crunching capabilities to support biology progress. We will see in the next chapter that Perlis and Snow are talking about the advantages in this first set.

- The second set is about *applying computing ideas in daily life*, completely apart from any use of computing. She talks about packing a backpack as an activity in which we might use insights from processor and device design (e.g., prefetching data before it's needed, and caching data for later use). She suggests that setting up a buffet or a graduation ceremony procession can be improved by using insights from design of processing pipelines.

The goal to develop computational thinking skills in students is worldwide. The new UK national curriculum for schools has computational thinking skills as one of the learning objectives. John Naughton in *The Guardian* described them in the following way [222].

Computer science involves a new way of thinking about problem-solving: it's called computational thinking, and it's about understanding the difference between human and artificial intelligence, as well as about thinking recursively, being alert to the need for prevention, detection and protection against risks, using abstraction and decomposition when tackling large tasks, and deploying heuristic reasoning, iteration and search to discover solutions to complex problems.

In Chapter 3, I revisit computational thinking. There is research support for the first set of claims in Wing's original definition. There is less support for the second set.

1.2.4 COMPUTATIONAL LITERACY

Computers are a new kind of tool, a new *medium*. Computers provide us with a new way to express ourselves. People understand new media and new tools in terms of old media and tools. The first silent movies were just recordings of plays, where the camera stayed still in a seat. That's how people understood motion pictures, in terms of plays. Cuts and pans all came later. A computer is a new tool, and we might start thinking about it in terms of older tools, like a printing press or a calculator.

Learning to use a new medium takes effort. The printing press was a huge leap in human history, but that leap didn't happen until many more people became *literate*. A printing press isn't much use unless your authors know how to write and your audience knows how to read [212]. Achieving *computational literacy* in society means that people can read and write with computation, which includes an ability to read and write computer programs.

A computer is more like a printing press than a calculator. The printing press made it possible to share words and pictures inexpensively with large numbers of people. That's how most of us think of the computer and the Internet. People use computers today for word-processing, presentations, or social media. Overall, the computer is a modern form of Gutenberg's printing press [212].

The creation of Gutenberg's printing press created a context for many different roles around textual literacy: reader, writer, printer, editor, distributor, and publisher. The computer as a kind of printing press creates many different kinds of roles, too. There are software writers (programmers, software engineers), readers (users), software manufacturers (e.g., Microsoft and Adobe), and software distributors.

The computer was invented explicitly as a kind of calculator to make complex computations faster and easier. Scientists, engineers, and business analysts use a computer to *calculate*. However, even those who calculate use the computer far more to *communicate* with than they do to process information. Scientists invented the World Wide Web to make it easier and cheaper for physicists to share information [22]. The computer is a medium by which people communicate even more than they calculate [102].

The goal of a computationally literate society is to be able to use computing as a form of expression and a way to think about domains other than computing. In many fields, computing allows people to do things that they could not without computing. Computational scientists and engineers use a new third way of doing science today. Science has been theoretical or empirical, but now can also be computational—using modeling and simulation to come to understand the world in a different way. Chapter 3 focuses on these goals. There are several research and intervention projects where the goal is to use computing to enhance other learning in schools [109, 276].

This idea of coding to learn, as opposed to learning to code, is captured by Mitchel Resnick and David Siegel in a 2015 article [262].

> We co-founded the Scratch Foundation in 2013 to support and promote a very different approach to coding. For us, coding is not a set of technical skills but a new type of literacy and personal expression, valuable for everyone, much like learning to write. We see coding as a new way for people to organize, express, and share their ideas.

1.2.5   PRODUCTIVITY

People who use the computer as a consumer (at the reader end of our printing press analogy) are referred to as *end-users*. Marshall McLuhan, the media theorist, suggested that we think about our media and tools as *amplifiers* of our basic human capacities [213]. The hammer amplifies our hand. The bicycle and the automobile amplify our legs—they do what our legs do but better (e.g., can carry more, can go further). Textual literacy gave us new ways to express and think, which led to significant advances [110]. The computer as printing press amplifies the voice of the end-user. The end-user can do and say more, which increases their productivity.

We know that a great many people will program as part of their jobs—far more than will be professional software developers. We call these people who are end-users of software, yet programmers, *end-user programmers*. A study in 1995 by Scaffidi, Shaw, and Myers attempted to estimate the number of end-user programmers. Their results suggest that, for every professional software developer, there are at least four end-user programmers—and possibly as many as nine, depending on how you define "programming" by end-users (e.g., is creating a spreadsheet programming?) [274].

It's harder to use the computer to be an end-user programmer than to be an end-user. Chapter 2 focuses on the challenges to learning programming. The benefit is worth the cost.

People who have made the effort to learn to use the computer as an end-user programmer are all *programmers*, but are not all professional software developers. You don't have to know how to build Facebook to gain from learning to program. Returning to the printing press and textual literacy analogies, knowing how to write means that you can write a letter to your grandmother, even if you can't write a novel.

People use computing not just because it saves them time, but because it allows them to think about their domains in new ways. In the text world, writers are not just amplifying their voices. Writers write to change themselves and how they think about their subjects. The cognitive psychologists Marlene Scardamalia and Carl Bereiter described this process in their book *The Psychology of Written Composition* [21]. Novice writers engage in a process of "knowledge telling." They simply report everything they know on a subject. More expert writers engage in a process of "knowledge transformation." The process of writing changes the way that the authors understand their knowledge [275]. The process of producing on the computing medium (programming) may also lead the end-user programmer to transform her understanding.

Many more people need to develop a notional machine, even if they don't become end-user programmers. There is a cost when people do not understand computing. Some of the colleagues with whom I've worked at Georgia Tech have documented everyday problems that come up because users don't understand computing.

- Brian Dorn's research on graphic designers identified examples of lost productivity [76]. Brian's participants did useless Google searches like `javascript file1` in order to find information about a JavaScript program that accessed a variable named `file1`. The end-user programmers that Brian was studying didn't know which variable or function names were meaningful and which were arbitrary, like the variable name `file1`. Brian saw one participant spend a half an hour studying a Web resource on Java, before Brian pointed out that he was programming in Javascript which was a different language. Because his graphic designers knew too little about computing, their searches were less productive, more flailing. There is a productivity cost in inefficient exploration time.

- Erika Poole documented participants failing at simple tasks (like editing Wikipedia pages) because they didn't understand basic computing ideas like IP addresses [250]. Her participants gave up on tasks and rebooted their computer, because they were afraid that someone would record their IP address. There is a productivity cost because users take action out of ignorance of basic computing concepts.

There is a long and wide spectrum from end-users to professional software developers who develop applications. These are all people who found power in being end-user programmers.

- There are historians who program to simulate the movements of people over time.

- There are graphic designers who automate tools like Adobe Photoshop or Gimp. By automating their processes, they get more work done in less time.

- There are end-user programmers who define little processes to do tedious tasks, like putting a bunch of pictures into a web page, or to reformat data for analysis in a spreadsheet. Alan Blackwell documented when home-owners decide to write a program to control some aspect of their home [26].

I have worked with biologists who use the computer to study gene sequences (e.g., to understand how related two gene sequences are), and others who use the computer to simulate populations (e.g., to understand disease propagation). They use completely different tools and methods. Those are two different and completely useful points within the user-programmer spectrum, within the same field.

The productivity argument for teaching computing to everyone has two parts to it. The first is that students can do so much more with computing. Just as computational scientists use computing to further their understanding, so can computer-using students. The second is that there is a cost in lost productivity when students make uninformed choices or thrash because they understand too little about computing. These arguments are similar to the ones that Alan Perlis and C.P. Snow made in 1961, which is described at the beginning of Chapter 3.

1.2.6 BROADENING PARTICIPATION

Most people who are in computing in the U.S. are male and are either of European descent (white/Caucasian) or Asian descent. At least 80% or more of those in computer science in the U.S. are male and white or Asian [134]. Less than 20% of students in undergraduate computer science programs in the U.S. are female or members of other ethnic/racial groups [46]. Less than 20% of technical employees in the computing industry are female or members of other ethnic/racial groups [211].

Take, for example, the Advanced Placement examination in Computer Science Level A. (Advanced Placement examinations are taken by high school students to gain credit or placement in U.S. universities and colleges.) The demographics of the students who take the AP CS exam are far different than the underlying high school student population. In general, the AP CS exam takers (in 2014) were less than 20% female, 3.9% African-American, and 8.7% Hispanic. We use AP CS exam demographics as an operational definition of the state of computing education in high schools in the U.S. There are certainly high school CS classes besides AP CS, but we don't have a way of measuring all of those. We use AP CS exam demographics as a dipstick, to get a sense of who is taking high school CS in the U.S.

These overwhelmingly male results are unique to computer science. Brian Danielak built this compelling visualization of Advanced Placement exam-takers in 2012 (Figure 1.1). Each dot represents one AP exam. The size of the dot indicates how many students took that exam. Placement in the middle horizontally means that the exam-taking is gender neutral. The dots are placed horizontally by a log-scale. You'll see most dots are on the right because AP exam-takers are in general more female than male. The leftmost dot (down at the bottom) is computer science.

Computer science is by far the most gender-skewed of any AP exam. The most female AP exam has far more male exam-takers than AP CS Level A has female.

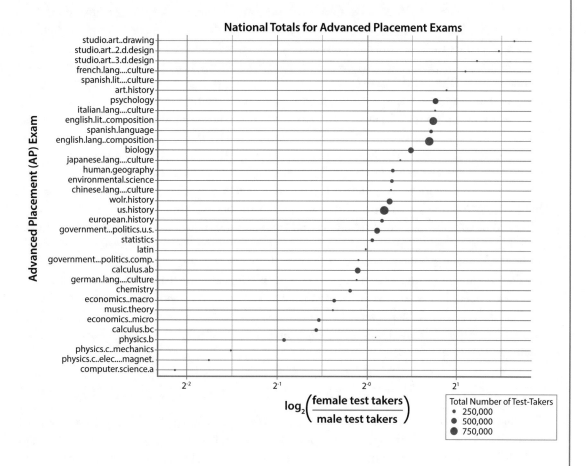

Figure 1.1: Visualization of gender among advanced placement exam takers in 2012 (courtesy of Brian Danielak).

Take the literacy lens on computing for a minute to get a different perspective. Swap those statistics out for another literacy. Imagine we said that only 20% of people who learned to read or to use mathematics were female. We would be understandably concerned that half our population was not gaining a literacy that we think is critical, and it raises the question why any form of expression should be so unbalanced with respect to gender or ethnic group.

As with any other form of expression, mastery of computing literacy has dramatic job impacts. If you don't know how to read, your job opportunities are limited. If you *do* know how to work with numbers, your job opportunities are expanded. If you know how to express yourself in computation, you have a skill very much in demand and you have access to some of the most lucrative jobs in modern economies.

The book *Stuck in the Shallow End* [203] presents a study of computing education in high schools in the Los Angeles Unified School District. Jane Margolis and her colleagues identified a range of factors that systemically prevented under-represented minorities from getting access to computing education. She described this as keeping students stuck in the shallow end of the economic pool. The better paying jobs are in the deep end, but without access to the skills to navigate that deeper end, they were stuck with lower paying jobs.

Margolis and her colleagues argue that access to computing education is a social justice issue. The demographics of computing are so skewed and the opportunities are so great. We have a moral obligation to provide those opportunities to a greater diversity of students.

There is not just one problem to fix to create greater access to computing education. Students from under-represented minority groups don't have access because there are so few teachers. There are few teachers because principals and administrators may think that their students are not interested in computing. Female students may not get access because of biases against them and their own sense of not-belonging. Since there are so few women in computer science, female CS students often report feeling a sense that they are "imposters." Some may feel that perhaps women just don't belong in computer science, and computer science is an all-boys club [204][15].

That belief has an enormous economic cost. We need to provide access to computing education to everyone, so that everyone has the opportunity to access these jobs. Currently, we overwhelmingly attract and retain men, white or Asian. How might we change how we teach to reach a broader population?

1.3   HOW DO WE TEACH COMPUTER SCIENCE NOW?

To achieve the goals described in the previous section, we will need to change how we teach computing. Most teaching of computing today occurs in higher-education. Most of that teaching is aimed at preparing programmers for the software industry. In order to describe how teaching should change, it's important to understand how we teach it now.

1.3.1   PERSPECTIVES OF COMPUTER SCIENCE TEACHERS

I have taught classes to Ph.D. students to help them become effective computing teachers, to faculty on how to improve their practice, and to high school teachers to develop their abilities as computer science teachers. When I'm teaching new computer science teachers, I often ask them to take the Teaching Perspectives Inventory.[2] It's a survey to help teachers understand their own perception of the goal of teaching. New teachers are often surprised that there is more than one perspective. They come to teaching with an expectation of what it's about, and rarely realize that others have a different expectation.

---

[2]See http://www.teachingperspectives.com/

Among the computer science teachers with whom I work, there are three perspectives that are most common. These are answers to the question, "What does it mean to be a good teacher?"

- *Apprenticeship perspective*: A good teacher in the apprenticeship model is a master programmer and usually has professional experience in software development. The teacher in the apprenticeship perspective is demonstrating expert practice. The student's job is to be an apprentice, model the practice of the teacher, and be coached in developing improved practice.

- *Transmission perspective*: Good teachers know the content very well, and know what is expected to be learned in a given course. The goal of the course is to match all the pre-requisites to achieve success in the next course. The goal of the teacher is to transmit the knowledge, and the goal of the student is to meet the course expectations.

- *Developmental perspective*: Good teaching starts from what the learner currently knows. A good teacher figures out what his or her students currently know, and then helps them improve their knowledge and skills. A good teacher is aware of common learning challenges and misconceptions, knows how to diagnose them, and helps students get past them.

The knowledge that is valued is different in each of these perspectives. The Apprenticeship model values knowledge of *skills and practice* the most. The Transmission model values knowledge of the *content area* above all else. The Developmental model values knowledge about *student development and misconceptions that challenge students* the most.

Each of these perspectives suggests different emphases in the classroom.

- Apprenticeship model teachers see the role of the teacher as demonstrating effective practice and as providing opportunities for the students to practice (with appropriate coaching). They focus their design on demonstrations and the design of homework assignments that give students appropriate practice.

- Transmission model teachers see the role of the teacher as providing the knowledge and insuring (through assessment and grades) that those who pass are prepared for the next levels. Transmission teachers worry about covering the content and exposing students to topics that are expected for a given course. In an educational system with a sequence of courses, they aim for students to meet the pre-requisites for the following course.

- Developmental teachers see the role of the teacher as being diagnostic (to determine what a given student understands) and providing attention to the needs of the individual learner. Since the teacher can't address everyone's needs, the developmental teacher designs learning opportunities so that individual students get what they need through peer instruction and other opportunities for active learning and social engagement.

An important point to realize is that these perspectives are not compatible with one another. In particular, the transmission and developmental perspectives can't both succeed in a single classroom assuming finite resources (e.g., the length of a given term, the hours available for homework, and the hours available for interaction with a teacher) and diverse students. If your goal is to transmit the knowledge of the course, you can't also spend time addressing individual students' needs that are far behind the average in your course. If you address each students' individual needs, you will be unlikely to have enough teaching resources to get everyone to achieve the same learning objectives by the end of the course. As educational researcher Benjamin Bloom pointed out, it makes no sense to expect all students to take the same amount of time (or other instructional resources) to achieve the same objectives [248].

The most common perspective I see among computer science teachers is an apprenticeship perspective. They see that their goal is to prepare students for jobs, and the most effective way of preparing students for those jobs is to have the students practice the skills and develop the conceptual knowledge of a practicing professional programmer. That makes sense if the learning objective is to become a software developer.

This book takes a developmental perspective. Cognitive science tells us that we have to start from where the learners are, as is discussed in Chapter 2. A transmission perspective is problematic in computer science education until we have more kinds of classes. There can't be only one goal for computing education. Our students are going to use computing for a much wider range of purposes than those of us who are computer scientists. Different students will see different purposes for learning computing. Not everyone will want to reach the far end of the spectrum from Facebook user to Facebook engineer. Identifying the knowledge that a broad range of students need is a theme in Chapters 3 and 4.

1.3.2   TEACHING FOR SOFTWARE DEVELOPMENT EXPERTISE

When computer science was first taught in schools, it was a novelty. Here was this remarkable new idea, a machine that could compute. Sometimes it was taught in mathematics, sometimes in electrical engineering, and sometimes it was in philosophy [84]. There was greater flexibility in teaching computer science in those days. Nobody knew just how significant the computer was going to be.

By 1968, the focus in CS teaching was clearly on *jobs*. The major curricular reports on computing came from the ACM (originally, the "Association for Computing Machinery"), the world's largest computing professional organization. The 1968 ACM Curriculum report [8] emphasizes the "demand for substantially increased numbers of persons to work in all areas of computing." The ACM report cited other reports (e.g., from the National Academy of Science) demanding more computing workers.

Why the change? Maybe it was then-Governor Ronald Reagan changing the country's expectation for higher education in the U.S. when he said on February 28, 1967 that the purpose of higher education was jobs [24], not "intellectual curiosity." Maybe it was the growing slice of the American economy that was dependent on computer hardware and software.

Nathan Ensmenger in his 2010 book *The Computer Boys Take Over* [84] argues that the culture of computing changed because the field discovered how difficult it was to produce good computer programmers and system designers. He suggests that much of the field of software engineering was invented to deal with the low-quality of most programmers. The field had too few high-quality programmers to meet the needs of a growing software industry. In a real sense, the field of software engineering was created because we were unable to solve the challenges of computing education.

Whatever the reason, computing education in the U.S. since 1968 has been focused on meeting the voracious needs for computing professionals to drive our modern economy. Learning computer science because it's a "rigorous academic discipline" (as the UK's *Computing at School* effort describes it today [30]) has ceased to be a goal in most computing education in the U.S. There is a tension in computing programs in today's schools between "fueling the tech economy" and broadening access to computing education for students who might not end up as software developers [216].

Computer science is classified as a *vocational skill* in most of the U.S. [107]. Literally, it's classified as *Career and Technical Education*, along with accounting and shop classes [133]. In many states, students interested in preparing themselves for college cannot take computer science classes for credit toward their secondary school completion. That classification places it in a different category than the rest of the science and mathematics courses classified as "STEM" (Science, Technology, Engineering, and Mathematics), a characterization that the U.S. federal government invented. In some states, Career and Technical Education is in an entirely different building than science and mathematics education. The teachers of computer science might not even see teachers of mathematics or science. What used to be taught together (as is described in Chapter 3) is now taught entirely separately.

1.3.3   EXPERTISE AND AUTHENTICITY ARE SOCIALLY DETERMINED

In the last decades, learning scientists have developed a recognition that social context is critical to understand how and what students learn. Few students are autodidacts who can read and learn just by reading many books, as did Matt Damon's character in *Good Will Hunting*. Rather, most students learn *to attain a goal*. Most often, that goal is defined in terms of *what people know and do*.

Jean Lave and Etienne Wenger [182], in their book *Situated Learning*, describe learning in terms of joining a social group. All learning is situated within activity, context, and culture. Students learn in order to join a *community of practice*. If you want to be an electrician or a plumber today, you still do become an apprentice and work with a master. The master is your example of someone in the center of the community of practice. You want to do things like what the master does. Moreover, you learn to value what the master values, as a model for the values of the community of practice that you want to join.

The way computer science is taught today is compatible with situated learning. We mostly teach computer science as an apprenticeship. Professional practice is a significant focus in determining what we teach [156]. We teach students to read and write code as software professionals do [196, 309].

Lave and Wenger are making a stronger claim than just describing how people learn trades and crafts in the modern world. They suggest that situated learning describes how *everyone* decides what is worth learning. A law student wants to be like expert lawyers and picks up values from what that student sees in the community of practice. A computer science student of the time of this writing values programming in Java and C++, using Agile methods, and dismisses as being low-value programming in languages like Pascal and COBOL because they are not in common practice.

Students want their instruction to be *authentic*. They don't want to feel patronized, like they are getting "toy" stuff. They want to be learning the real stuff. But what's authentic? Education researchers have shown that there are several senses of authenticity [281]. Maybe it's using the same tools that experts use. Maybe it's evaluating student work to the standards of experts. It might also be using the same processes as experts.

The important point in all of these is that authenticity is measured compared to "experts." But these probably aren't all the same experts for all students. Lave and Wenger point out that we compare ourselves to experts who are in the community of practice that we hope to join.

For students who don't aim to be professional software developers, the experts are harder to define. Some students may be comparing themselves to expert programmers—perhaps because they don't know what programming looks like when used by experts in their domain. Other students may be aware of what programming looks like in their domain. Students who want to program in computational science or graphical designer communities (for example) may reject learning Java and Agile methods, for good reasons.

The issue of authenticity is an important theme in this book. Sometimes, you can construct a sense of authenticity [136]. Within the same class, each student's sense of authenticity can vary depending on their future career goals. Computing teachers need to consider authenticity when teaching. If the students don't know the values and skills of their community of practice, the teacher will need to convince the students that the topics of the course are authentic (what Reed Stevens calls *accountable disciplinary knowledge* [304]).

1.3.4   THE INVERSE LAKE WOBEGON EFFECT

To a large extent, what we know about teaching computing to our current students is not useful when trying to understand how to teach computing to everyone. Most of what we know about teaching computer science is from studies at the undergraduate level [97], who are a select group of students who passed admissions standards. Even at the high school level, computer science education is mostly available to students in the middle- and upper-income brackets. What we know about teaching computing education is mostly from teaching privileged students.

We know little about teaching the broad range of students. Elementary and high school students are mostly filled with students who will not go on to college, at least in the U.S. We have little research about teaching students who are below average in intelligence or who have special needs [208].

When we make assumptions about teaching computer science to everyone based on our experiences in teaching computing education, we might be making biased decisions based on the *inverse Lake Wobegon effect*. The *Lake Wobegon* effect is "a natural human tendency to overestimate one's capabilities" [171], so-named for the mythical town of Lake Wobegon where "all the children are above average." This is a common cognitive bias. For example, 80% of drivers believe that they are above average drivers. We believe that what we experience (small sample) is exceptional.

The inverse Lake Wobegon effect is seeing only a small exceptional sample and believing that it represents the whole. In computing education research focused on undergraduates, we may believe that we are studying *average* students, but in reality, we only see the students who truly are "above average." Post-secondary students have to be admitted to college or university. That selection process biases the sample—colleges and universities don't see everyone. Consider a successful introductory computer science course at a university in which 80% of the students are successful. Since most universities in the U.S. only take students in the top half of ability, that same approach may fail for 60% of the general population. Studying undergraduate computer science learning does not tell us what it will be like to teach computing to everyone.

We need much more research in computing education to understand how to teach everyone. We don't know how expensive it will be to teach everyone and what problems will arise. We don't know what computing can be taught to students with special needs.

1.4   HOW SHOULD WE TEACH COMPUTING FOR EVERYONE?

The previous sections describe the broad range of reasons for making computing education available to everyone. The last section described how computing education works today. In this section, I consider how we might re-design computing education for everyone.

1.4.1   LEARNER-CENTERED DESIGN

In 1994, Elliot Soloway, Ken Hay, and I suggested that *learner-centered design* (LCD) was different than what most designers do when creating user interfaces for software [295]. The most common user interface design approach, *user-centered system design*, emphasizes understanding the user's tasks and helping her to achieve those tasks [230]. User-centered system design led to interfaces that made users more efficient in their tasks.

The practice of user-centered system design assumed that users were experts in the tasks in which they were engaged. Learners aren't experts, so designing for them is different.

1. Learners don't know the domain (the conceptual and procedural knowledge associated with an activity or discipline) or the task. That's the point of being learners.

2. Each learner has a variety of motivations. She may not be *opposed* to learning the domain or the task, but that's not necessarily her top priority. (She may be opposed to becoming a programmer, however, as described in Chapters 5 and 6.)

3. Learners are different, each with their own set of motivations. Users working on the same task are more alike one another than, say, students thrown into the same classroom.

4. Learners don't stay the same for long. What works for them on Day 1 probably won't work well for them on Day 100.

User-centered system design didn't start as an approach to making interfaces better for experts. The emphasis on asking the users about their tasks moved it that way. In a similar way, computing education is predominantly about preparing students to be expert professional software developers. We ask industrial experts what we ought to teach our computer science undergraduates. We use industrial practices to determine our curriculum content. If we are going to teach computing to everyone, we will have to change what we teach and how we teach it.

Learner-centered design is a starting point. The most critical idea in learner-centered design is respect for the learner. Learner-centered design tells us to respect students motivations to learn and what they want to learn. We expect variety in our learners and rapid change as they learn. We need to construct learning opportunities for who the *learner* is and wants to be, not for the *expert* that we computer scientists might want them to be.

Learner-centered design also tells us explicitly where to begin with re-designing computing education. We have to begin by understanding the learner. Introspection is insufficient. Not everyone wants to be a computer scientist, a computing education researcher, or a computing educator. Our motivations and the communities of practice that matter to us are unlikely to be the motivations and the communities of practice of interest to our students. We have to start with research.

1.4.2   EXAMPLE: COMPUTATIONAL MEDIA AT GEORGIA TECH

We can design computing education that works for a broader range of students than just those who excel at computer science today. We can make curriculum that engages a more diverse community of learners. I have several examples throughout the book, and mention one here.

At Georgia Tech we created a second undergraduate computing major, a *B.S. in Computational Media*. The Computational Media program is the only cross-college joint undergraduate degree at Georgia Tech. Students in Computational Media are in both the College of Computing and our School of Literature, Media, and Communications in our Ivan Allen College of Liberal

Arts [48]. Half of the required classes for students in Computational Media are traditional computer science classes, the same computer science classes that our B.S. in Computer Science majors take. The other half of the classes are from the Literature, Media, and Communications school. These are classes in visual design, interaction design, film history, performance art, and similar classes that place technology in a cultural and design context.

Changing the content of what we are teaching changes who is engaged in the classes. While the B.S. in Computer Science at Georgia Tech has a student population of less than 20% female, the B.S. in Computational Media (with the same computer science classes) is now over 40% female. Our Computational Media *graduating* classes are also over 40% female, so we *retain* as well as *engage* the female students. The B.S. in Computational Media is an accredited computing degree program that is nearly gender-balanced [127].

Students who graduate with degrees in Computational Media go on to join video game companies, computer animation companies, and web design and advertising companies. Some do become professional software developers. Some even go on to graduate studies in computer science.

Computational Media succeeded in drawing in a more diverse range of students because it supported a wider range of target communities of practice. Computational Media is about more than being a professional software developer. It's also about narrative, design, and gaming. Supporting a wider range of target occupations is supporting a wider range of communities of practice that students might want to join. Supporting a wider range of possibilities can provide more ladders into the pool and the skills to stay afloat in the deep end.

1.5   OVERVIEW OF THE BOOK

The purpose of this book is to provide an overview of the research on how to teach computing to everyone. In this chapter, I presented reasons for teaching computing to everyone, and the current state of how we teach computing. I used learner-centered design as a starting point for thinking about changing computing education to meet everyone's needs.

In Chapter 2, I consider the challenges of learning programming. Not all goals for broad computing education include programming. Most of our research in computing education is about programming, and as I point out at the beginning of the chapter, programming may be our best way to help students develop a notional machine.

Chapters 3 through 6 consider different populations of learners, and these are summarized in Table 1.1. For each population, I ask what community of practice the learners want to join and what learning goals they might have. In each chapter, I consider the teaching methods that might help students in that population achieve those goals and join that community of practice.

- Chapter 3 considers the goal of using computing as a tool to support learning in other domains, including the goals of computational thinking. One of the student populations in this chapter is STEM students. Their goal is to be educated citizens and workers, who can use physics, mathematics, and STEM problem-solving skills in their lives. For these students, much of the research has emphasized programming as a medium. Programs are a notation that expresses causality and time better than traditional mathematics.

- Chapter 4 is about teaching computing to non-CS majors at the undergraduate level. I focus on liberal arts, architecture, and business students in the example of *Media Computation*. I describe how it was designed and the results over the last decade [121, 126]. The general teaching method being used is contextualization which is teaching computing in an application context that makes it authentic to the learners.

- Chapter 5 is about adult learners. I consider two groups of adult learners that we have studied in my research group: graphic designers and high school teachers. Graphic designers are already in a community of practice—of artists, not programmers. They want to learn programming in order to enhance their productivity and to create new opportunities. They do not want to lose the creativity and enjoyment that they find in their profession. The teaching method we use is to embed computing education in their work materials. Teachers are also members of a community of practice of teachers, but to be successful computing teachers, we need them to become members of a community of practice of computing teachers. The learning goal, then, is to develop a new identity as a computing teacher, which requires confidence in their ability to teach computing, knowledge about computing and programming explicitly, and knowledge about teaching computing, called *pedagogical content knowledge*. They need efficient, low cognitive load activities.

- Chapter 6 is about computer science majors who want to join a computing professionals community of practice, but not all as professional software developers. In this chapter, I describe how we need to change our teaching for a broad set of careers in the computing industry. These techniques include contextualization, offering choice, and using more active learning methods (such as peer instruction and pair programming).

In Chapter 7, I reconsider the goals of teaching computing education listed at the beginning of this chapter. For each of elementary school, secondary school, and higher-education, I consider how and what we teach to achieve the goals of computing education for everyone. I also consider the economic cost of computing education for everyone. It may be too expensive to teach today in the way we want students to learn in the future.

Table 1.1: Summary of book in terms of student audience, the community of practice they hope to join, their learning goals, and the teaching methods described in the chapter

Learners	Community of Practice	Learning Goals	Teaching Methods
Students studying STEM (Chapter 3)	Educated citizens and workers	Physics, mathematics, problem-solving skills	Programming as notation, as medium
Liberal arts, business, and architecture students (Chapter 4)	Professionals who use computing for communications, and less for calculations	Creative expression with computing; understanding computing in their lives	Contextualization: media computation
Graphic designers (Chapter 5)	Artists (not programmers)	Productivity, creative opportunities, enjoyment	Embedding computing education in work materials.
High school teachers (Chapter 5)	Teachers (typically not in CS, but need/want in CS)	Identity: Confidence, pedagogical content knowledge, programming knowledge.	Efficient, low-cognitive load activities
CS majors (Chapter 6)	Software industry	Programming knowledge (sometimes software development expertise.)	Contextualization; choice (e.g., threads); active learning methods— peer instruction, pair programming

CHAPTER 2

The Challenges of Learning Programming

If programming was easy to learn, there wouldn't be much challenge to computing education. Since programming requires the programmer to have a robust notional machine, then we could simply teach programming, and we would achieve all the goals described in Chapter 1. The problem is that it's hard to learn programming.

In this chapter, I review what we know about the challenges in learning programming. The story starts with empirical evidence of the challenge of learning and teaching computing. Next, I present results from learning sciences on how learning works, so that we can use those insights to understand how to improve computing education. Finally, I offer two theoretical perspectives that provide insight into computing for everyone: situated learning and expectancy-value theory.

2.1 THE RAINFALL PROBLEM: PROGRAMMING IS HARDER THAN WE THOUGHT

In the 1980's, Elliot Soloway's group at Yale began capturing all the programs written by computer science students. The students were writing in a programming language called Pascal [154], a notation for writing computer programs that was explicitly invented to be good for teaching students. Student performance on one particular problem intrigued Elliot and his students [294]. Here was one form of that problem.

> Problem: Read in integers that represent daily rainfall, and print out the average daily rainfall. If the input value of rainfall is less than zero, prompt the user for a new rainfall. When you read in 99999, print out the average of the positive integers that were input other than 99999.

Students were expected to write a program that would accept numbers as input from a user at the keyboard. The students had to infer what variables would be needed to solve this problem and the combination of things to keep in mind at each step. Each number would be added to a running *total* of all the numbers read, and a *count* would be kept of the number of input numbers, so that the average could be printed at the end. If a negative number was input, that should be considered a mistake. The program should not add the number to the total, and the count should not be incremented, but the program should go on to read more numbers. If the input number was *99999*, then the program should stop reading numbers, and shouldn't add that number to the total, and shouldn't increment the count. Then, print out the average.

This doesn't seem like an unreasonable task for a Yale Computer Science student. This problem wasn't computing the next prime number after 1000, or computing the 10,000th digit of pi, or writing a program for Tetris or Angry Birds. However, this was a surprisingly difficult task.

- When Elliot's group gave this task to the first-term computer science students (about week 12 of a 16-week semester), only 14% of the students got it right [293]. Getting the programming language wrong wasn't the issue—syntax errors were ignored in this analysis. Most often students had trouble *not* adding in the negative or end numbers, or they didn't consider troublesome cases, e.g., what if *only* negative numbers were input?

- Elliot's group also gave this task to students in their *second* CS course, in the same 12th week of a 16-week semester. Now, 36% of the students got it right.

- Finally, Elliot's group gave the task to students in an advanced Systems Programming course, where everyone was a Junior or Senior (3rd or 4th year). 69% of the students got it right. Not 100%, for a problem that seems reasonable to give to first-year students.

Elliot's Ph.D. students did a lot of work with the Rainfall Problem. Lewis Johnson wrote his dissertation about *Proust* [155], a system that could successfully diagnose problems in student programs like "You added the negative number into the total." Jim Spohrer developed a model that explained what errors students would make with the Rainfall Problem, and it matched the empirical student data well [300].

One possible explanation for the difficulty was the programming language and how programming was taught in that language. Elliot and his group published one study where they modified the programming language Pascal [293]. A correct solution to the Rainfall Problem in Pascal had a general structure that looked like this:

```
Read (the number)
Repeat as long as the read number is valid
      Process (the number, e.g., is it negative? 99,999?)
      Read (the NEXT number)
```

In this solution, the program reads a number before the loop, then inside the loop, processes one number then reads the next number. Elliot and his student added the ability to give up the repetition early, using a `leave` statement. In modern languages like Java and Python, this is called a `break` statement. In this new *Pascal-L*, students could write a program like this:

```
Repeat forever
      Read (a number)
      Test (the number, and if it's 99,999, LEAVE the repeat)
      Process (the number)
```

Students were far more successful with Pascal-L than with Pascal. With Pascal-L, 96% of the advanced undergraduates got a form of the Rainfall Problem correct—much as you would expect for a problem that seems like it should be easy for novices. This was an early indication that students had cognitive preferences for certain programming strategies, and if the programming language did not support those strategies, the task was made harder.

2.2   MULTI-INSTITUTIONAL, MULTI-NATIONAL STUDIES

Elliot Soloway's group wrote papers and dissertations describing the challenges that students had with programming. Mike McCracken realized that few were listening. Computer science teachers easily dismiss research results about computing education [14]. Maybe it was just Yale and how they taught computer science. Maybe the results could be easily dismissed with, "Well, that's the problem of using Pascal—we should use a programming language more common in industry." Pascal did fade from common use, in favor of languages in industrial practice [146]. A choice for a language in industrial practice is a choice for greater professional authenticity.

In 2001, McCracken organized the first multi-institutional, multi-national (MIMN) study of computer science [207]. His idea was to ask students to complete the same programming task at several institutions in different countries using different programming languages. If students did well, then maybe Elliot's results were just Yale or Pascal. If they did not, then we had a big research question that generalized across all those institutional contexts. MIMN has become an important research design in computing education research [96].

The task that McCracken posed was simple, "Build a calculator." Students were to read input numbers or operations, and they could use any ordering of operations and numbers, e.g., 3 + 2 or 3 2 + or + 3 2. Five institutions in four countries participated, and an international team did the assessment and evaluation, known as the *McCracken Working Group* (MWG). The evaluation team used a grading rubric to score the students' work. Out of a possible 110 points, the average score was 22.89. One teacher actually "cheated" and lectured on how to build a calculator before his students attempted the problem. There was no difference in scores between his students and the others.

Clearly the problem wasn't Yale or Pascal, but there were still critics of the MWG study. Maybe the problem was too hard. Maybe it was too much to ask students to *design* and *program* the calculator.

Raymond Lister gathered a new MIMN working group in 2004 [196]. His idea was to focus just on *reading* and *tracing* code, not on design. Rather than an open-ended task, his team built multiple choice questions. The first set asked students to *trace* code, i.e., figure out what the computer would do when asked to execute those instructions. Students had to predict the output of short pieces of code. The second set of questions presented short pieces of code with pieces missing, a desired output, and a set of possible lines to insert into the missing pieces. Students had to choose the lines that completed the program correctly. Over 900 students participated in some portion of the study, from 12 institutions from 8 countries, with over 550 students completing the full multiple choice question instrument. Average performance was 60%. The conclusion of the study was as follows.

> Many students were weak at these tasks, especially the latter (filling in code) task, suggesting that such students have a fragile grasp of skills that are a pre-requisite for problem-solving.

In 2013, more than 10 years after the original MWG, a second MIMN McCracken working group was formed to revisit the original study [319]. The 2013 MWG study involved over 400 first-year CS students at 12 institutions in 10 countries. The task was simpler in the second study.

> Students were asked to complete the implementation of a class (called Time) representing a 24-hour clock. The behavior of the clock with respect to wrap-around of the hours, minutes and seconds values was described with examples. The clock has four operations which students were asked to implement: a tick operation which advances the stored time by one second, a comparison operation which determines the order of two times, and add and subtract methods which calculate the sum or difference of two time values.

Performance was better than in the original MWG. 75% of the students got the tick operation right, 73% got the comparison working, but only 65% got time addition working and 61% got time subtraction working. Those are not stellar results on a problem that everyone agreed should be well within the range of performance for a first-year CS student. But this time, no one was surprised. The second MWG ended their report with:

> It may be that the longest-lasting effect of the original MWG has been to depress teachers' expectations of their students' ability!

2.3   MEASURING COMPUTER SCIENCE KNOWLEDGE

When computing teachers argue about changing strategies in the introductory course (e.g., choosing a new language, or a new curriculum), they often ask, "But will students learn the same as they did before the change?" There is a significant fear than an approach that makes learning easier may not help students to learn the same. In terms of teaching perspectives, this is a tension between a Transmission and a Developmental perspective. Allison Elliott Tew was interested in measuring these differences between different approaches to teaching introductory computer science. Does it matter if we use Pascal or Python or Java, or any of the other dozen programming languages in common use in introductory courses? Does the curriculum matter?

She did a study where she focused on students entering their second computer science class [317]. These students came from different introductory classes at Georgia Tech. (The different classes are described in Chapter 4.) Allison developed two *isomorphic* tests of knowledge from the first and second classes. Her two isomorphic tests were meant to test the exact same things in the exact same ways, but the problems differed in small ways. For example, one problem might require computing an average of a set of numbers, but the numbers would be different on the two tests. Allison gave one of those tests at the beginning of the second class, and another at the end of the second class.

She found that students from different classes performed very differently on the first test. She could clearly see who took which kinds of classes, and the strengths and weaknesses of each of those classes. But on the second test at the end of the second class, all the differences went away. She could no longer tell who came from which introductory class. Students whose classes were weaker in some dimension caught up by the end of the second class.

This was a great result! If the differences disappear within a single 15-week class, we need not worry about what programming language or curriculum we use in the first class. Allison repeated the study over the following semesters—and never found it again. In every repeated study, there were still differences in the second test.

Allison considered her study critically. Maybe the problem was in the instrument that she was using. Was she sure that the two tests were isomorphic? Was she sure that the knowledge she was asking about was covered in both the first and second courses? Is it all the same knowledge every semester? What if "CS105" (some random CS class) covers topic X (say, how to test if a number is negative) in detail with lots of practice one semester, but puts more emphasis on topic Y (e.g., how to leave a loop when you've reached the end of the input numbers) the next semester. If she asks about X in her test, then students from the same class (but different semesters) could be reasonably expected to understand topic X differently. If topic X is fundamental to understanding topic Y, those students from the "same" class could similarly be expected to learn differently in the second class.

Allison wrote her dissertation on her development of the first language-independent, validated test of introductory computer science knowledge. The language independent part was important because she wanted to be able to test across different languages. Her process is an exploration of what we mean when we think about "learning introductory computer science."

First, she had to come up with a definition of "What's the knowledge we expect in introductory computer science at the undergraduate level?" The introductory CS undergraduate course is often referred to as *CS1*. Some researchers have tried to answer that question by asking experts to rank topics. She decided to take an empirical approach by getting the top textbooks used in CS classes, then identifying common topics in those books (e.g., toss out topics that only appeared in one textbook). The list of topics was too huge to build a test around, so she used curriculum recommendations to whittle the list down further—what do professional organizations say is the knowledge that introductory courses ought to have? Finally, she asked a panel of experts to help her identify the most critical items from her list of CS1 topics. She ended up with 10 constructs that serve as the basis for her test: fundamentals (variables, assignments, and expressions); logical operators; testing and selecting alternatives (e.g., if statements); definite loops (for loops);

indefinite loops (`while` loops); arrays; functions and methods with parameters; functions and methods with return values; recursion; and object-oriented basics (e.g., reading a class definition, and calling methods on an object) [315].

Next, she developed her multiple choice questions. For most of the topics on her list, she aimed to create three questions. First, she asked students to show that they understood the *definition* of the topic. Her second and third types of questions were directly taken from Raymond Lister's working group. She asked students to show that they could *trace* programs that used the construct, and that they could use the construct to *fill-in code* where there were empty lines in a program.

The tough part about building good multiple choice questions is defining the distractors. What are the wrong answers that you put into the question that will distract the students who don't really know the right answer? Allison created open-ended versions of her questions (e.g., not multiple choice) where students had to provide an answer, and she built the questions in three different programming languages in common use in introductory computing classes: Python, Java, and MATLAB (a common programming language in Engineering). She then asked students to answer these questions in a *think-aloud setting*, and she asked students to talk about what they were thinking when they worked on the question. By using a think-aloud approach, she could test the wording of the questions. Did students read the questions the way she meant them to be read? Some students got the questions right, but many got them wrong. One of her most interesting results was that the top three *wrong* answers for each question were surprisingly consistent across programming languages. Maybe student understanding and *misunderstanding* of computing was about the same across languages. She now had questions with good distractors [312].

She created four tests with the same problems. She created one test for each of the programming languages Python, Java, and MATLAB. She created a fourth test in a *pseudocode*, i.e., a programming language of her own invention that was like those other languages, but not exactly like any of them. Her hypothesis was that students taking the pseudocode version of her test would perform about the same as they would in the test in the programming language they learned in class.

Allison then conducted the largest study ever of introductory computer science students. She had 950 participants at three institutions in two countries each take two versions of the test. Everyone took the pseudocode test, and everyone took the same test in the programming language of their course. Half the participants took the pseudocode test first and half took the native language (the one taught into their introductory course) test first, and then a week later, they swapped.

Her test was successful [316]. She found that the correlation between the pseudocode test and the native language test was high and statistically significant (e.g., it was unlikely to be due to chance that she happened to get about 1000 strange students). For measurement purposes, the pseudocode test (which she now called the *Foundational CS1 Assessment* (FCS1)) was identical to the native language tests. She also correlated the students' final exam scores in their introductory classes with her pseudocode test, which also correlated highly. That final test showed that her whole assessment process did result in a measure essentially the same as the course overall. She really did test the knowledge of CS1 for those students.

The final word on FCS1 ties back to the previous section. A good assessment tool should not have most people doing very well, what educational researchers call a *ceiling effect*. If the average score is 90%, then there's not much room for measuring differences between different curricula, for example. FCS1 was designed to be a test on only the most fundamental, the most common parts of CS1 classes. The average score on FCS1 was 33.78%.

The Rainfall Problem, the McCracken and Lister Working Groups, Tew's FCS1—these studies suggest that most students who take CS1 do not learn the content of CS1.

2.4 HOW LEARNING WORKS

The psychology of learning is not a required subject for computer scientists, even those who teach computer science. Understanding how learning works in general gives us a starting place for understanding how learning works in computing. That understanding helps us in addressing student challenges when they learn computing.

2.4.1 ASSIMILATION AND ACCOMODATION

Learning in computer science or any other subject is about adding content (concepts and procedures) to our memory. Human memory works by association [70]. We associate or connect ideas to one another. When we are in a situation where we want to remember something, we use characteristics of our situation to seek the information we want.

Learning is a conscious process of sense-making. We encounter some novel information, and we add an association to our memory about the novel information in a way that makes sense, i.e., fits with our existing network of associations. Jean Piaget first identified two processes by which these associations enter memory, *assimilation* and *accommodation* [159]. Assimilation is the process by which new memories get added to existing networks. You know that U.S. states have capital cities, and then the novel information you find is that Augusta is the capital of Maine. You can simply add that association to memory. Accommodation is when you realize that the way you thought about the world does not work for the new memory. You have to change the way that your network of associations are structured in order to accept the new information. When a learner first realizes that objects fall because of gravity, and it's not because air pressure is pushing down on them, the learner must accommodate.

There is an affective component to this, too. Students have to consciously try to make sense of the novel information. They have to want to learn the novel information [175]. Learning scientists are concerned with *appropriation* which is the process by which learners develop a relationship with knowledge, a sense of ownership over it, and develop an identity as someone who is literate in that knowledge [159].

Associations are created in our long-term memory through our working memory, which is sometimes called short-term memory which highlights one of its limitations [70]. Working memory is transient, and it's also limited in size. We can only attend to a few items at once, and only for a short while. If constructing an association for long-term memory requires the learner to combine too many items at once, or items across time, then we say that the learning has high *cognitive load*. High cognitive load can inhibit learning. It's just too hard to attend to all the things needed to make sense of the situation.

We recall information by following connections until we reach the desired information. The process of *activating* new knowledge based on the current situation works in parallel—whole sections of memory get triggered at once, which activates other knowledge. If you can't remember something, that doesn't mean that you don't have the information in your memory. Since information is accessed by following connections, not remembering may mean that you can't get there from here. You may not recognize the information you need in terms of the situation (current stimuli) in front of you.

2.4.2   TRANSFER OF KNOWLEDGE

The problem of learners having knowledge that they can't use was first identified by Alfred North Whitehead in the 1920's, and he called it *inert knowledge* [322]. Whitehead noted students who learned the content well enough to pass examinations and a course, but seemed to forget all the information immediately after the course. Today, we'd explain that as students associating all the knowledge about the course with *only* the course itself. When the situation was *European History 101*, students might remember everything that they learned for the class *European History 101*. But if they found themselves on the streets of Oxford, England, looking at the monument to the religious martyrs, they might not recall ever learning about religious martyrs in England. If someone was to remind them that they learned about religious martyrs in *European History 101*, they might be able to access the information. In general, though, we would say that their knowledge of European History was inert, even *brittle* (i.e., it's good for one thing and one thing only, answering a test). Inert knowledge is a useless form of knowledge if it is only used when taking tests.

When a student *knows* something, but seems unable to access that information in a new context, we say that there is a lack of *knowledge transfer*. Students who can acquire knowledge in one task or situation and then apply it in a different one are transferring knowledge [229]. Students who passed the test but can't seem to write programs with that knowledge are demonstrating an inability to transfer knowledge.

Experts often teach abstract and formal rules as a way to achieve transfer. Rules like $F = ma$ apply literally everywhere. The problem is that students don't know or see that the rules apply everywhere [269, 270]. Students see only the surface level features of problems, so they don't think about the abstract and formal rules because they don't connect the context of the situation to the formalisms [181]. Students need to see many concrete examples before they can start to abstract away the surface level details and see the underlying principles that transfer across examples [277].

Computing education researchers have known for many years about transfer problems. Back in 1976, Ben Shneiderman observed that learning a second programming language was sometimes *harder* than learning the first [283]. John Anderson and his colleagues noted that students' knowledge of computer science is tightly tied to the way that their first programming language looks and feels [6]. If the second language that they learn is radically different, they have to go to the effort of generalizing their knowledge. Calling a method in Lisp *looks* different than calling a method in Java, even though the underlying mechanisms are similar. Students see surface features.

We can use even this little bit of knowledge about learning to help us answer the question at the end of Section 2.3. Why did students do so poorly on the McCracken Working Group challenges?

- Maybe the students did not learn as much computing as we might expect in a first course. There are lots of reasons why learning might be inefficient or ineffective. Perhaps the teacher mostly lectured, when active learning would have led to less inert knowledge [105].

- Maybe the students do not recognize the problem as related to anything that they did before. That would be a failure to transfer. There are ways that we can explicitly teach for transfer, to help students to see how to use what they know to solve novel problems [176].

- Maybe the problem is far harder than we realize. My colleagues Briana Morrison and Lauren Margelieux were unsuccessful in replicating some basic educational psychology experiments using introductory programming problems [218]. Their hypothesis is that the cognitive load of the problems is just too high.

2.5   WHY DO STUDENTS LEARN LESS COMPUTER SCIENCE THAN WE EXPECT?

What are students learning when they learn computer science and programming? Why can't they solve these seemingly simple problems? An obvious answer is that these are not simple problems. We have an expert blind spot that makes it difficult for us to see what students do not understand [221]. Developing a greater understanding of the challenges for computing students requires us to apply lessons from the *learning sciences*. Learning sciences grew out of the cognitive science and artificial intelligence in education communities, with a particular focus on practical impacts on education systems. Learning sciences is a broad umbrella that overlaps much of education and educational psychology [273].

We can safely assume that students who receive a passing grade in an introductory computer science course are learning something about computer science. People are always learning. Learning results from trying to make sense of the world. People learn when they encounter something they don't know or understand, but want to know or understand. However, they might not be learning what the teacher wants, or in the way that the teacher wants.

When students can't solve problems that seem simple and should be easily solved for someone who passed the course, we realize that this learning challenge is more complicated than we might have thought. Maybe the students were not motivated to try to understand. Maybe they learned instead how to pass a class without learning anything about computer science.

2.5.1   WHAT MAKES LEARNING COMPUTER SCIENCE DIFFERENT

Are introductory computer science classes harder than comparable classes in mathematics or other science areas? I believe it is harder to get started in computer science than in mathematics or science. While students likely have a lot of experience with computers before they enter their first computer science classroom, they likely have no experience with telling the computer what to do (programming). While students may have experience providing directions or instructions to other human beings, they likely have never given instructions to a machine using an unambiguous notation. When students enter the biology, chemistry, and physics classrooms, they arrive with a dozen years or more of experience in a world filled with chemical, physical, and living things. Students enter the computer science classroom never having had the opportunity to see the computing under their applications.

A significant source of student errors in learning programming is *negative transfer* from communication in a natural language to coding in a programming language [233]. We enter the computer science classroom with years of experience communicating with other human beings. What we type into the computer looks like natural language. But the computer is not human. Roy Pea calls this class of bugs the *superbug* [244]:

> The default strategy that there is a hidden mind somewhere in the programming language that has intelligent interpretive powers.

We use language to communicate between human beings, who have some shared experience of the world. We use programming languages to communicate with beings that have no experience of the world at all. Even more confusing, we use words like `for` and `print` and even `and` in common between the natural and programming languages, but they don't have *exactly* the same meaning. In our natural communication, the human that we're communicating with can infer some of our meaning from context, even if not all of the words are understandable. Not so with computers, and that is a significant source of difficulty for early programmers.

The computer is never trying to understand the programming. The computer is merely doing what it has been told to do. Humans almost never do that.

2.5.2   DEVELOPING A NOTIONAL MACHINE

The need for a notional machine is a significant difference between computer science and other STEM disciplines. In computer science, students can do almost nothing without a notional machine. Developing a notional machine is significantly different than learning to solve other kinds of STEM problems.

In many areas of mathematics and science, students can get started solving problems by rote. Students can look at a problem at a surface-level, figure out the variables of interest, and plug them into well-defined formulas [181]. Physics students can look at the problem of dropping a rock from a two-story building, plug values into $x = x_0 + vt + \frac{1}{2}at^2$ and figure out the time it will take the rock to fall—even before they really understand how acceleration due to gravity influences vertical velocity [282]. Students can compute the length of a hypotenuse without understanding the proof of the Pythagorean Theorem. Calculus students can compute derivatives and integrals without understanding the fundamental theorem of calculus.

In computer science, we work with programs that are executed by a computer, not with equations. Bruce Sherin studied this difference in physics. He showed that equations are great for helping students understand *balance*—you change one variable, and the other variables change in response. A computer program requires you to think about *causality*, because things happen step-by-step, and actions on one line influence what happens on later lines.

Sherin had one group of students learn physics using equations, while another group learned physics with programs written in a language designed for learning called Boxer (which appears again in Chapter 3). Sherin had students use programs to explore the relationship between position, velocity, and acceleration. For example, he had students work with code that looked like this (paraphrased):

```
for each time step:
    make the velocity the sum of current vertical velocity + acceleration
    make the Y position the sum of the current Y position + vertical velocity
    move to the new position
```

Sherin found that his students learning programs understood better how acceleration *influenced* velocity, which *influenced* position. (An image of this Boxer program can be seen in the next chapter as Figure 3.3.) The Boxer program wasn't just an equation. The Boxer-using students learned a causal mental model of physics. The program in Boxer was a better medium for learning about causation, but was not as effective for understanding the balance that equations could represent. If a physics teacher wants students to develop a causal, step-by-step mental model of physics, a program is a better medium for representing that mental model than an equation.

To succeed in introductory computer science classes, students have to be able to build *mental models* of what the computer is doing when it reads and executes the program [197]. As mentioned in Chapter 1, Benedict duBoulay called this mental model of a computer the *notional machine* [78]. An exceptional article for understanding the challenges of developing a notional machine is Juha Sorva's 2013 paper [298].

The notional machine is unnatural for us. The inhumanness of computers makes them harder to understand. Computers execute programs—quickly, literally, and mercilessly. A simple typing error can lead to a drastically different program than the one that was intended. The computer is a non-human agent that is doing what was specified, and not what was intended. Realizing that the computer has its own agency, that it will do what it was told to do, and won't work with you to figure it out is a significant challenge, especially for younger students [260].

The student facing a program that *she* wrote, that isn't doing what she meant it to do, must figure out what *this* program is doing. She has to find the mistakes that have to be fixed to turn the program into what was *intended*. This process is called *debugging*, and it's necessary from the very first program that a student writes in computer science class—at least, the first one with any typos in it. The challenging of debugging is like being placed in a physical world where motion follows the equation $x = x_0 + 2vt + 4at^2$ (i.e., swapping the constant 4 for our world's $\frac{1}{2}$), and we have to figure out the difference from this world from our world by dropping rocks. Imagine solving this challenge in your first physics class with limited knowledge about physics methods of measuring time and distance. That's what debugging in the first computing class is like.

It's particularly challenging to develop a notional machine because the computer's process is invisible—memory is not visible, the computer executing instructions is invisible. One of the most common strategies for communicating the notional machine to students is the use of visualization [299]. If we could show a picture of what the computer is doing when the program runs so that it is no longer invisible, perhaps the students could understand the program better. Juha Sorva studied students using a visualization of what the computer is doing when it ran their program, and a significant percentage of students found that the visualization just made things more confusing [297]. Now there was this program over here, and these pictures over there, and the correspondence wasn't obvious. The same problem has been seen in many algorithm visualization systems [149]. Visualization can play a role in helping students develop a notional machine, but it's not obvious nor automatic.

Students invent stories for themselves about how different programming language features work, and some of these stories are wrong [100]. The *assignment statement* is one of the simplest and most basic parts of any programming language. Here is an example:

```
a = b
```

That statement means (in the most common programming languages), "copy the value that's in the variable b and put it in the variable a." It's not a statement about mathematical truth. Rather, the assignment statement specifies an *action* that the computer has to take. Computing education researchers have catalogued a variety of ways that students get that simple statement wrong [28, 297]. Sometimes students tell themselves that that statement copies the value from a into b (reversing the meaning). A more common misconception is that the value in b gets *moved* into a, and b now contains nothing at all. Another common misconception is that we have now created a *relationship* between a and b, so if the value of b is ever changed, then the value of a will be automatically updated to match.

One of the challenges for higher-education teachers is that they have significant expertise in computer science. They don't see these flawed interpretations of the assignment statement.

They have an *expert blind spot*. Teachers tend to make decisions based on their *content knowledge* over the knowledge that they have about good teaching in the domain (called *pedagogical content knowledge (PCK)* [148]) [221]. Once you see how computers work, it's hard to "not-see" how computers work. It's hard to see with the novices' eyes. It's hard for expert computer scientists to see the students' misconceptions, but it's critical. We know that being able to identify student misconceptions is a hallmark of expert teaching [272].

We can be aware of the expert blind spot when thinking about how we learn to read. Once you know how to read, you can't see "A" as two vertical slanting lines with a horizontal line, as you did before you knew your letters. You see a capital letter "A." You can't look at the word "cat" and see $c - a - t$ anymore—you automatically and uncontrollably read the word cat. That's why empirical research is so necessary for developing effective teaching practices. We get past our expert blind spot by carefully studying how students see things.

2.6   INCREASING THE VALUE OF LEARNING COMPUTING

My colleagues Amy Bruckman and Betsy DiSalvo published a paper with a terrific quote [62]:

> Computer science is not that difficult but wanting to learn it is.

If programming is inherently hard to learn, we might be able to improve learning in computer science by making it more motivating, by making it more worthwhile. Much of the rest of the book is about efforts to increase student motivation to learn computing. By figuring out what the student wants to learn and what will motivate her, we can more effectively design learning for the student.

In my research group we draw on two theories for understanding how to motivate learning in computer science. The first one appeared briefly in Section 1.3.3, *situated learning*. The second is *expectancy–value theory*.

2.6.1   SITUATED LEARNING

Situated learning [182] says that learning is motivated by a student's desire to join a community of practice. Students don't just want to study history or biology. They want to become part of a community of people who use history or biology, like being a teacher or a doctor or a nurse. They study in order to join that community. People at the center of that community of practice have other reasons for learning, but most people are in a process of becoming, of developing an identity as someone in that community. According to situated learning, we will motivate student learning if students understand why what they're learning will help them achieve their goals.

Educational psychologist Patricia Alexander has a *model of domain learning* which meshes with situated learning [4]. Few students are interested in the domain (like history, biology, or computer science) for its own sake until they have significant knowledge and expertise. All students start out with limited individual knowledge in the domain. Their *situational interest* is sparked by the environment. Social pressure, the context in which the domain is presented, wanting what's needed to get necessary certification, and wanting to be like the experts in the field can provide motivation for novices. That initial spark can lead to *competence*, which can eventually lead to *proficiency*, but it's only at the proficiency level that students are interested in the domain for its own sake. It makes sense—it's hard to fall in love with a field until you know it.

Situated learning helps to explain why we can't fix ills in the computing industry through teaching. Sometimes, practitioners will suggest "we can get programmers to use this paradigm (e.g., object-oriented programming), if we just teach it to them from the start," or "most programmers have these bad coding habits, so let's teach students to program differently from the first class." That doesn't really work because students want to learn what's really used. Students want to know what is in authentic practice. They're not interested in learning the things that aren't being used yet. They want to join the community of practice, not create a new kind of practice. If you want to change the community of practice, one reading of situated learning suggests that you get the practitioners at the center of the community to change what they do. The rest of the community will change to follow them.

2.6.2 EXPECTANCY-VALUE THEORY

Why do so few students (especially women and under-represented minority students) choose to pursue computer science? In general, how do students make academic choices? Jacqueline Eccles and her colleagues developed an *expectancy-value model of achievement motivation* [320] that helps to explain how students make academic choices. Expectancy-value theories explain how people are motivated to make choices based on the expected outcome of the choice. Academic choices include, "Should I pursue this field of study?" The Eccles model (Figure 2.1) talks about "children" but is more broadly about "learners." The role of the *socializer* may be different with adults, but the influence chain is likely similar.

The Eccles model says that some of the things that students take into consideration are the following.

- Cultural Milieu: Do people like me (by gender, by race or cultural group, by other aspects of identity) do things like this?

- Expectation of Success: Could I succeed at this?

- Child's Interpretations of Experience: Have I done things like this and liked it? Have I been good at it?

- Subjective Task Value: Do I want to learn this? What's the incentive to do this? What's the cost?

The lines in Figure 2.1 describe influences, which have been developed through regression analyses [82]. The influences can help us understand what we can influence directly and what has indirect influences. For example, what the socializer (e.g., teacher, parent, mentor) wants for

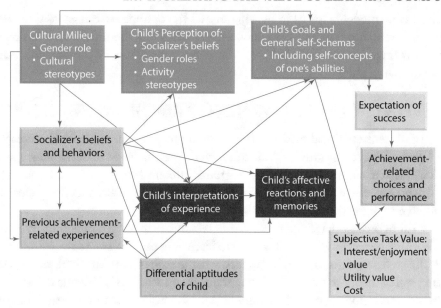

Figure 2.1: Eccles' model of academic achievement (adapted from [320]).

the child doesn't directly influence the student's choice. Rather, the socializer's beliefs influence the students' self-beliefs, which influence expectations for success, which influence the choice. A student's belief about whether or not she can succeed at something is a significant fact in influencing academic choices.

The Eccles model is helpful for understanding why there are so few women and students from under-represented groups (e.g., in the U.S., African Americans and Latinos/as) in computer science. Students are less likely to study CS if they don't see people like them succeeding in CS, if they don't see value in learning computing, if they don't see that they will be welcomed, or if they don't think it fits into their view of themselves in their community [81]. Just telling them that "it's for you" is one kind of "Socializer's beliefs" that are trying to influence the student's perceptions, but there are so many other kinds of beliefs and cultural influences on students. All of these influence the student's goals and expectations of whether she can succeed at computing.

Sometimes the value of a model like Figure 2.1 is useful when realizing what it says about what is *unlikely* to work. Significant effort in the U.S. is focused on telling students what great jobs there are in computer science. In Eccles' model, those messages aim to influence the bottom right factor in the model, the subjective task value. The goal is to increase the utility of the choice. However, that message does nothing to influence student expectations of success, which is the other significant factor on student choice. If students still don't think that they belong in CS, or that CS is too hard, they are unlikely to pursue computing academic choices, even if the jobs are lucrative [80].

The Eccles model helps us in figuring out all the options we can explore to change those decisions. We can show students role models. We can show them that they can be successful. We can show them how valuable it is. We can make it more fun. A combination is likely to be necessary to change students' decisions.

2.7   WHAT MAKES LEARNING PROGRAMMING HARD

We have significant empirical evidence that learning to program is harder than teachers might predict. Some of the reasons that it's difficult include the challenge of developing a notional machine. A notional machine is what makes programs different from equations. It makes computing powerful as an expressive notation, but makes more demands on the student—especially because it is so foreign to our experience.

Critical to success in learning computing is wanting to learn computing. We can motivate student learning by teaching what they want to learn. We can determine the community of practice that the student wants to join, then teach what is authentic to that community. We can use expectancy-value theory to understand the influences on students' academic decision-making.

In the next chapter, I consider computational literacy as a reason to learn computing. Different than the jobs argument, the computational literacy argument suggests that computing has value for everyone, even if they never take a computing or STEM job.

CHAPTER 3

Computational Thinking and Using Programming to Learn

The last chapter described the challenges that learners face in learning to program. Situated learning and expectancy-value theory suggest how we might be able to make programming more valuable and attractive to learn. The focus of this chapter is about those benefits of learning programming. For over 50 years researchers have argued that learning programming has transfer effects—although we are still challenged to find them. Learning programming might still be a path to learning, even without the transfer argument. Computing is a powerful medium, and programming is a powerful notation. Learning how to use this medium to facilitate expression and learning (i.e., computational literacy) is an important reason for learning to program.

3.1   COMPUTERS AND THE WORLD OF THE FUTURE

1961 is the earliest that I've seen the argument that everyone should learn to program, and not because it was important for a job. The argument was made twice, by two influential thinkers. One offered a carrot. The other offered a stick.

In 1961, the MIT Sloan School held a symposium on "Computers and the World of the Future." Martin Greenberger edited a remarkable volume with transcripts of all the lectures, as well as all the discussion afterward [115] (see Figure 3.1). Not only were the speakers remarkable, but their discussants have had significant impact on today's world as well.

One of the speakers was Alan Perlis, who was literally one of the people who named the new field "computer science." Perlis explicitly argued for teaching computer science to everyone on every university campus. He defined computer science as the study of process, and argued that specifying processes, comparing processes, and proving characteristics of processes impacts every discipline on campus. The computer offered the opportunity to automate process, which created enormous new opportunities. Perlis wanted everyone to learn programming, to give them the notation for processes and the power to automate process.

He was challenged on this point by Peter Elias, then the chair of Electrical Engineering at MIT. Elias suggested that programming would one day be unnecessary, because the computer would figure out what the programmer wanted. Perlis suggests that Elias missed the point.

"Perhaps I may have been misunderstood as to the purpose of my proposed first course in programming. It is not to teach people how to program a specific computer, nor is

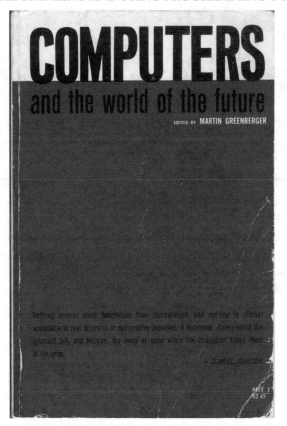

Figure 3.1: Scan of my well-used copy of *Computers and the World of the Future*.

it to teach some new languages. The purpose of a course in programming is to teach people how to construct and analyze processes. I know of no course that the student gets in his first year in a university that has this as its sole purpose."

"This, to me, is the whole importance of a course in programming. It is a simulation. The point is not to teach the students how to use Algol, or how to program the 704. These are of little direct value. The point is to make the students construct complex processes out of simple ones (and this is always present in programming), in the hope that the basic concepts and abilities will rub off. A properly designed programming course will develop these abilities better than any other course."

Worth mentioning is J.C.R. Licklider's response to Elias's comments. Licklider had the original vision for the Internet, and he was the program manager who funded the development of the original nodes on the Internet. Like Elias, Licklider was one of the discussants for Perlis. He responded with another kind of carrot, a McLuhan-esque argument for the power of the medium.

> "Pete, I think the first apes who tried to talk with one another decided that learning language was a dreadful bore. They hoped that a few apes would work the thing out so the rest could avoid the bother. But some people write poetry in the language we speak. Perhaps better poetry will be written in the language of digital computers of the future than has ever been written in English."

Perlis explained in his lecture how being able to build models and simulations changes a field dramatically. He talked about researchers at Carnegie Tech (before Carnegie Mellon University) running experiments that you couldn't do in the real world. Perlis predicted modern computational science and engineering and its enormous value, which is remarkable for 1961. Learning programming gives everyone access to the enormous power of being able to create models of their world and ask questions through simulations. Perlis offered the carrot of what students can achieve if everyone learns to program.

C.P. Snow showed us the stick. Snow was a British science advisor during World War II. Based on that experience, he wrote the book *The Two Cultures* [291] where he described the split he saw between the humanities and science views of the world. He argued that scientists needed to understand more of the moral and cultural issues that the humanities perspective offered, and he critiqued humanities scholars for not appreciating the power and insights of science. Snow saw a similar split because too few people learn computing.

Snow predicted that algorithms would soon rule the world. He argued that those who do not understand how programs are written are at the mercy of those who do. He talked about the importance of understanding *algorithms*, which is a description of the process that the computer follows in a program. Snow described those algorithm writers:

> On their own, outside of the review of others, they will be making decisions in secret that will be impacting our lives at the deepest level.

Snow was remarkably prescient. Algorithms like the Google page rank algorithm and how credit scores are computed have dramatic impacts on our lives. Those who don't understand algorithms are at a disadvantage for understanding how the algorithms influence their lives.

Both Snow and Perlis are talking about the importance of understanding computing for every citizen. They are not talking about meeting labor needs in technology. They are talking about what everyone needs to know about technology to give them access to enormous power and to understand how their world is controlled.

3.2   COMPUTATIONAL THINKING

One of the reasons for teaching computing to everyone listed in Chapter 1 is computational thinking. Jeannette Wing suggested that learning computing provides new kinds of insights, skills, and concepts that could be applied in other domains. She gave several examples, which I separated into two sets. The first set is about *applying computing ideas to facilitate computing work in other disciplines*. The second set is about *applying computing ideas in daily life*, completely apart from any use of computing.

The challenge to computational thinking is the problem of knowledge transfer. If you learn to make a computer repeat steps, does that influence how you think about your co-workers, as Jeannette Wing suggests [326]? If you learn how to sort numbers with recursion, do you also learn how to use recursion when developing a strategy for tiling your kitchen floor?

What we know about knowledge transfer suggests that it's quite hard to get transfer from one area of computing to another. For example, I showed evidence in the last chapter that students fail to apply even simple computing ideas to fairly simple problems. A set of learning activities have been designed for students called *CS Unplugged* which aim to teach computing concepts away from the computer. Researchers found that students doing these activities rarely connected them with computing [307]. Even learning activities designed to teach computing might not get connected to computing.

Achieving the goals of *applying computing ideas to facilitate computing work in other disciplines* is clearly achievable. This is what Perlis was describing in his 1961 lecture. The notation of programming is powerful for describing models, as Bruce Sherin described (in the last chapter). Computer science has many important principles that have influenced many disciplines [56]. Students gain tremendously in productivity and in access to jobs by learning computer science in ways that encourage application to their fields and careers.

Applying computing ideas in daily life is less likely. The odds that students will transfer their knowledge from computer science class into the world outside are low. To my knowledge, there has not been a study since Wing's 2006 paper that has successfully demonstrated that students in a computer science class transferred knowledge from that class into their daily lives. It's hard to demonstrate transfer. Students might say (self-report) how they planned to use computing in their daily lives [49]. Self-report does not mean that they actually change their problem-solving behavior to use computing outside of a computing context. In Ann Brown's famous 1992 paper on design experiments [29], she described how difficult it was to get students to apply general cognitive or higher-order thinking skills training to improve learning. Students rarely applied the lessons outside of an experiment's prompting and did not spontaneously transfer the knowledge. Ann Brown was explicitly teaching these students skills and still rarely saw any transfer.

The only way that we know to achieve knowledge transfer is to teach for transfer. We can teach students how to tile their kitchen recursively, for example. We probably can't teach much about computer science at the same time, with a fixed amount of resources and time. In the next section, I review some of the efforts to use programming as a tool for learning.

3.3   PROGRAMMING AS A TOOL FOR LEARNING

Seymour Papert proposed in his seminal 1981 book *Mindstorms* [238] that we could use computing to create a "Mathland." Papert believed that students would learn mathematics well if they were immersed in a world where they could construct mathematics, play with mathematics, and use a mathematical language. His language for children to play with mathematics was Logo. Papert believed that when students made a mistake (a *bug*) in their Logo programs, it would likely reflect a mistake in their thinking about the underlying mathematics. When they fixed the mistake (*debugged* the program), they would be correcting their own thinking—debugging their own understanding.

Papert was describing a process for how interaction with programming could transform the way the programmer thought about the domain of the program. The process he described is much like what Bereiter and Scardamalia had also seen working when a writer interacted with her text [21]. The process of creating the artifact created the opportunity to think about the domain in a new way.

Papert believed that this perspective went beyond mathematics. He argued that we could use Logo across the curriculum, so that it could connect to many different disciplines [237, 239]. The same model would work across disciplines, of debugging the programming to correct the understanding within the discipline. One interpretation of Papert's idea is that students would be learning generalizable higher-order thinking skills from learning to program Logo. By generalizing this model of working out ideas in Logo code, students would learn some general problem-solving skills. They would learn to debug in their real life better.

Papert aimed to re-imagine mathematics using computation as the medium. He invented a *Turtle Geometry* as a way to introduce geometry to students in an accessible manner using the power of a computational medium. Unlike Cartesian coordinates which require an external frame of reference, turtle geometry is limited to a relative frame of reference. The turtle can move forward (`fd`), turn right (`rt`) by a certain number of degrees, and can execute combinations of these commands (and a few others) (see Figure 3.2). Papert made turtle geometry *body syntonic* [238]. The student can move her own body to match the movements of the turtle to trace the program concretely. While turtle geometry is accessible, it's also surprisingly powerful. Abelson and diSessa wrote the book *Turtle Geometry* to use this accessible system for describing biological simulations, spherical coordinate systems, and even Einstein's Special Theory of Relativity [2].

3.3.1   SMALLTALK AND BOXER

The quest to create the computer as a tool for learning has dramatically shaped the modern world of computing. Alan Kay visited with Papert and took these ideas in a slightly different direction, a more McLuhan-informed direction [170]. Kay realized that the computer was humanity's first *meta-medium*. The computer could be prose or poetry, music, sketches, animation, or just about any other medium. What's more, the computer could respond to the human being, and thus, create something entirely new while being able to represent everything old. Alan didn't believe

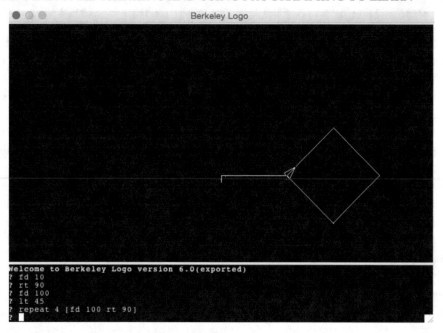

Figure 3.2: Commanding the turtle to move in Logo.

that Logo was sufficient to realize this goal. He didn't believe that current computing hardware was sufficient to realize this goal, either.

Kay created a vision for the hardware and software platform on which humans could use computing for learning and expression. He called that vision a *Dynabook* [169]. In pursuit of that vision, Kay and his team at the Xerox Palo Alto Research Center (PARC) invented the Smalltalk programming language, object-oriented programming, and the desktop user interface (e.g., overlapping windows, icons, menus, and a mouse pointing device). Quite literally, the modern personal computer was invented on the path to the Dynabook.

Andrea diSessa's vision focused on creating opportunities to support *computational literacy*, as an analogue to language literacy [65]. diSessa worked with Papert at MIT on Logo. Like Kay and Papert, diSessa believed in the power of computing to transform learning and expression. diSessa's *computational literacy* saw students learning to express themselves in computation from kindergarten through adult, and using computation to solve problems and explore ideas. Like Kay, diSessa felt that Logo was insufficient to achieve these goals.

Boxer was diSessa's successor to Logo which featured novel interface ideas like *naive realism*, or the principle of "concreteness" [66]. Variables and other data structures appear in Boxer as visual boxes (Figure 3.3[1]). There are no invisible data structures hidden in memory. Everything

[1]Used with author's permission.

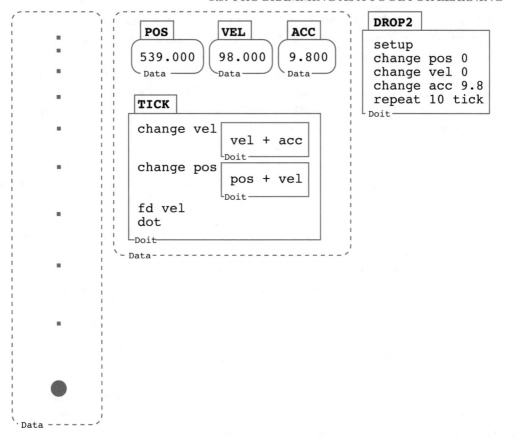

Figure 3.3: Boxer running one of Bruce Sherin's example Physics programs (adapted from [282]).

can be visually inspected and manipulated. diSessa believed that Boxer would be easier to get started with than Logo and would be capable of doing more. In Boxer, students could do object-oriented programming and network programming—it was capable of more modern and advanced computing than Logo [67]. diSessa and his students used Boxer in a variety of domains, from inventing new graphing representations to learning physics [68, 282].

3.3.2 STUDENTS BUILDING SOFTWARE TO LEARN

One of the most powerful examples of using Logo to create an immersive Mathland was developed in Idit Harel's dissertation work [137]. Harel invented the *Instructional Software Design Project (ISDP)*. She asked 4th graders (around 9 years old) to build software to teach 3rd graders (around 8 years old) about fractions. She conducted a comparative study where she had two groups of 4th graders, one developing Logo software and one that had additional math instruction for the same amount of time. At the end of the study, the software-building 4th graders performed better than the comparison 4th graders in both knowledge about computer science and Logo and knowledge about fractions.

Harel believed that there was a real synergy between the mathematics and the programming, and the motivation to teach others both inspired the 4th grader's effort and got them to think about the fractions content. What's hard about fractions? How should we represent fractions to make them more understandable?

The idea goes beyond fractions. Yasmin Kafai extended the ISDP idea [158]. She continued working in the same school in the following year so that the (now) 5th graders could serve as "consultants" to the (new) 4th graders who were building computer games to teach fractions to 3rd graders. Kafai created a community of learners where students talked about fractions and writing programs, so that new kinds of collaborative learning opportunities were created.

Kafai expanded the model into science, and had students build software to teach and demonstrate ideas in science [161]. She found that the students didn't always learn a lot about computer science or programming, even when they were learning science. Sometimes, they did not use particularly sophisticated code because they didn't really need anything all that sophisticated to teach the mathematics or science ideas that the students wanted to present.

Over the years, Kafai has had students build in order to learn in a variety of media for a variety of learning purposes. She has students construct video games [164], craftwork [163], and e-textiles [279]. She has shown how students have learned mathematics, science, and other subjects like art [247] using computation.

My own dissertation work is connected to this story. I asked students to program physics simulations, as a way to learn about both physics and computer science—very much like the ISDP model that Harel and Kafai were exploring. I created a programming environment, *Emile*, where students would build falling, launching, and racing objects [118]. They implemented loops that manipulated position, velocity, and acceleration, just as in Bruce Sherin's studies in Boxer.

Emile was notable for featuring *adaptable software-realized scaffolding*. Scaffolding is the term for supports that a teacher or parent might provide to enable a student to complete a process that she would be unlikely to complete without the support [327]. Scaffolding is supposed to *fade* (i.e., to change or even disappear), but most software-realized scaffolding does not [142]. Learner-centered design tells us to expect that students change [295], so the scaffolding must be adaptable to still be useful to students as they change.

Like Boxer and Smalltalk, Emile was an exploration of how a programming environment for learning might be different. There were supports built into the software to make the programming easier to do, but slower and more constrained. For example, when process supports were on, students had to do things in a particular order. Students started out programming by combining *action plans* (chunks of code that achieved a particular goal) from a *Plan Library*, and the plans could be specialized for the particular situation by filling (typed) *slots* in the code (see Figure 3.4). But they could turn that off and just type code if they wanted.

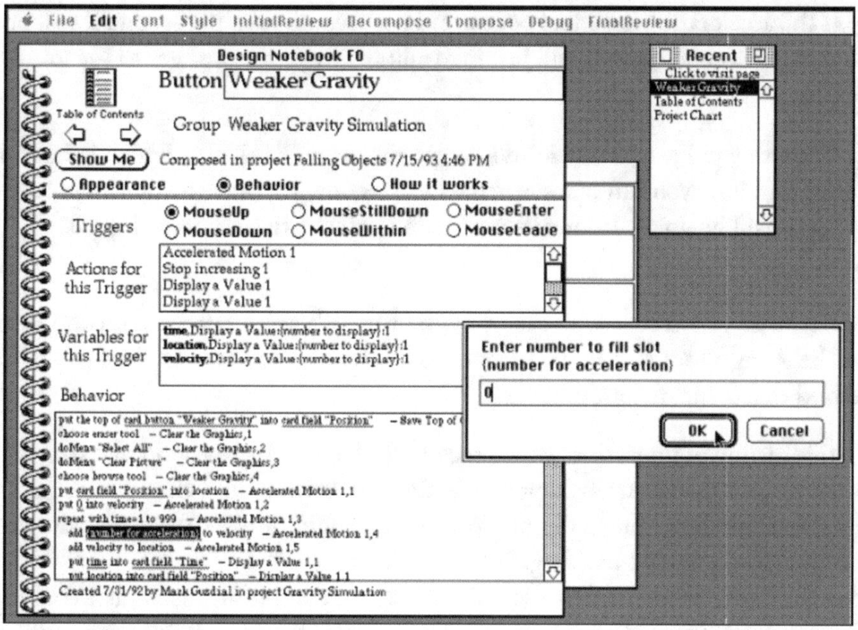

Figure 3.4: Filling a slot in a plan in Emile.

The idea was that students would be allowed to turn on and off these supports (scaffolding). Students did turn on the scaffolding when working on something new or difficult, then turn it off when they knew what they were doing and wanted to just race ahead. Students would turn on the plans supports when they wanted to grab a bunch of things from the library and have support in connecting them to their existing code, and then turn them off to type code around them.

The performance of students using Emile looked more like Kafai's science students and less like Harel's fractions students. Students using Emile to build physics simulations gained a new understanding of physics ideas like *velocity* and *acceleration*. At the beginning and at the end of the workshop, I interviewed the students and asked them questions like, "If you left your seat right here and right now, and went to the ice cream store up on the corner, would you need to accelerate to make it there in 10 seconds?" and "If you dropped a rock off the top of this three story building, how long would it take to hit the ground" On the pre-test, students demonstrated only naive models of physics. But on the post-tests, some students demonstrated causal, moment-by-moment models of physics, like Sherin's Boxer-using students [282].

Researcher: Can you tell me how long it took the rock to get to the ground?

Student B: It would be about one second

R: Okay, where did you get that from?

B: If the acceleration is 30 feet per second per second, then per second it will be going 30 feet per second, then it will just take a little longer for it to get to the ground.

R: Why?

B: Because you have to divide the, to get the average velocity, which is how fast it's going, and how you can measure how far it's gone, you have to…let's see…it will be going, it will be going 15 meters per second. Maybe two seconds, I guess.

R: Why?

B: Because…1.5 seconds. Because, by the time it's accelerated the second second, it will be going about 45 feet per second, so it'll have to be between the first and second second that it hits the ground.

In this section of transcript, we can see the student tracing the loop that simulated projectile motion. He talks through what happens in the first second, and then the second second. He learned a causal model of projectile motion that he could transfer from the computer screen to talk about rocks falling off a building.

But the Emile students didn't learn much about computing, as far as I could tell. When I showed them screenshots of simulations like those that they had built, they could not describe how those simulations might be working any better at the end of the workshop than at the first. Maybe they didn't need to learn much CS to be successful with their simulations. Maybe I asked the wrong questions when inquiring about their CS knowledge. Maybe the "teaching someone else" motivation of ISDP was critical. I suspect that part of the problem was a time issue. Harel and Kafai had students work over months. The Emile study was a three-week summer course. It likely takes more time to learn enough of the programming *and* the context domain to see and develop synergies between them. Scardamalia and Bereiter suggested that writers have to have a certain level of expertise before the act of writing transforms the writer [21]. We should expect that even end-user programmers must develop certain expertise with the medium before they can develop a synergy between programming and the domain.

3.4   PROGRAMMING AND PROBLEM-SOLVING SKILLS

Many teachers of Logo believed that their students were learning generalizable higher-order thinking skills by using Logo. They believed that Logo was helping their students think and learn better. Even today, it's an open research question if that can happen. The evidence we have suggests that it probably has not been happening.

In the 1980's, soon after Papert's *Mindstorms* was published, Roy Pea and Midian Kurland and their colleagues studied a group of Logo-using students [245, 246]. They found no evidence that students were gaining higher-order thinking skills. To be fair, they did not see much evidence that the students learned programming [179]. The students were not writing sophisticated programs, and perhaps not surprisingly, did not learn much computer science. But the Pea and

Kurland papers were the death knell of Logo in schools [231]. Within just a few years, Logo all but disappeared.

A significant meta-review in the *Review of Education Research* looked at studies on the relationship between learning programming and problem-solving skills [235]. The conclusion was that researchers had no evidence that there was any connection. Just as Ann Brown described [29], students rarely apply generalized learning and thinking strategies. Learning to program did not lead to students spontaneously transferring knowledge from computing to everyday life. Most studies, however, ran up against the same problem as Pea and Kurland. Most students do not really learn much computer science in their computer science classes.

We do have evidence that we can teach problem-solving skills using programming. Sharon Carver did a remarkable study where she used Logo programming to teach students how to debug similar kinds of problems (e.g., arranging furniture, delivering trees, or visiting airports or running errands) [38, 173]. She wanted students to figure out, for example, where the instructions go wrong and don't get you to the destination, by tracing on the map.

Carver created a detailed model of exactly what skills she wanted students to gain. She created her model so that the skills would work for both tracing Logo programs and for tracing other kinds of directions.

Her model had five phases.

- *Program evaluation.* Run the program. Compare the program plan and the program output. If they don't match perfectly, use the next four phases.

- *Identify the bug.* Describe the difference between the plan and the output. Use the list of specific types of bugs to figure out which is the most likely.

- *Program representation.* Use the representation of the structure of the program to identify probable locations of the bug.

- *Bug location.* Use the cues from the last two phases to locate the bug.

- *Bug correction.* Replace the bug with the correction, and try again.

She then taught her debugging model with Logo, using both turtle graphics and list processing. Her students successfully transferred the skills to non-programming tasks. She did not teach programming and then discover that the students gained problem-solving skills. Instead, she decided what problem-solving skills to teach, and only taught enough programming in order to teach those problem-solving skills [39].

The lesson from Carver's work is that we can achieve transfer by teaching the skills we want to transfer. Carver showed that programming is a good medium for teaching those skills. In terms of our reasons for teaching computing to everyone, this is more about computational literacy and productivity. Computing is a powerful tool for learning. Programming itself is unlikely to lead to transfer of problem-solving skill.

3.5   LEARNING PROGRAMMING TO LEARN MATHEMATICS AND SCIENCE

What the computing education research literature suggests is that programming can be a powerful medium for learning mathematics and science. It does not happen by accident. Learning programming does not make you into a great problem-solver, mathematician, or physicist.

Students have to learn their computer science quite well to expect much transfer of knowledge. Recall Allison Elliott Tew's measurement of CS knowledge from the previous chapter. Tew looked at the correlation between how the students performed in their class and the difference between how they performed on the pseudocode test and on their course language test. She found that the difference was smallest for the best students, and grew as the students did worse in the class. Her interpretation was that if you knew computer science well, you could transfer the knowledge well from your CS course to the pseudocode test. If you don't know CS particularly well, you struggle in mapping ideas from your course to the pseudocode test.

In Chapter 1, I suggested that we think of the computer as a kind of printing press, in that it creates a context for a new kind of literacy. I mentioned the work of Scardamalia and Bereiter who showed that the process of writing changed the writer's understanding of the topic of the writing [21]. We can reasonably expect the same thing might happen with programming. Writing a program to solve an engineering problem may give students new insights into the engineering problem. Writing a program to express an idea can transform how the programmer thinks about that idea. This is not about transfer. This is about the power of using a new medium, of applying computing to new domains.

We can design for transfer to happen, as Carver did, but we cannot simply expect it. Changing how people generally view their world or solve problems does not come cheaply. We can design for students to learn something else using programming as a medium. We know more about how to achieve learning *through* programming.

- If you want students to use programming to learn something else, develop a model of what will be needed to learn something else (like Carver) then limit how much programming you use. Only use the parts of programming that you need for the something related that you're trying to teach.

- Design specialized programming environments explicitly to make it easier to learn the programming in order to learn something else. Like Emile, this will likely require scaffolding.

- Learning both programming and some subjects (like mathematics or physics) may create some synergy. Learning both together may take less time than learning each separately, because there may be concepts in common (like variables). However, learning both certainly will take more time than learning only one. *Give students a significant amount of time to learn both the programming and the subject*, or reduce expectations of either the programming or the subject. How much time is an open research question, but will likely depend significantly on the prior background of the learner.

That's how Bruce Sherin used Boxer to teach kinematics [282]. Boxer was explicitly designed to be easy to get started with, even easier than Logo. Sherin used only a subset of Boxer programming. Sherin found that students learned things using programming as the medium of Physics expression that were more difficult to learn with equations.

A similar approach is being used to teach other parts of science. Uri Wilensky and Michael Horn teach computer science within high school science classes [323]. Standards for science education include students creating models of the world and then learning through exploring computer executable models. Wilensky and Horn point out that that's computer science, exactly as Alan Perlis proposed in 1961. They have teachers teach using a specialized form of Logo, called *NetLogo*, that is easier to use for science learning and has more sophisticated features than the Logo of Papert's time. Because they only use a portion of programming and computer science, they can teach teachers how to do this relatively easily (e.g., they can start teaching with programming with fewer hours of professional development) [323]. Irene Lee uses the same general approach with middle school science in her Project GUTS (Growing Up Thinking Scientifically) [184]. She only teaches a small amount of programming, using a specialized environment (StarLogo, a cousin of NetLogo), to teach science.

The Bootstrap project is about learning mathematics with programming [276]. Algebra is an important subject for students to go on in mathematics, but is very difficult for many students [94]. The Bootstrap team teaches algebra by having students build video games, with a programming language (Racket) in which variables and functions work just as they do in algebra. They use a specialized programming environment, called *WeScheme* [332], that is simplified for use by students. They don't cover all of Racket—they use just enough to be able to teach ideas like linear equations and distance calculations in a compelling context like building video games. They explicitly teach a problem-solving process that transfers from programming in Racket to work in algebra. Their results suggest that students are learning algebra through programming [276].

3.6 LEARNING ABOUT COMPUTER SCIENCE WHEN DEVELOPING COMPUTATIONAL LITERACY

The common thread across all of these successful projects using programming to teach mathematics or science is that students are learning a small core of programming that applies in the other domain. Students are learning a set of generative concepts that can be combined in powerful ways. As Perlis said, being able to automate process changes everything in other domains. Students can learn using computing to automate process with only a small set of programming principles—they don't have to develop the skills of a professional software developer.

Most of the studies of the projects using computer science to teach something else have focused on the learning of the something else. Where the learning of computer science has been studied, there wasn't a whole lot learned. But maybe because we were looking in the wrong place.

As we think about learning computational thinking skills, we can focus at a different level. Rather than asking if students are gaining knowledge of the programming language and the skills of a software developer, we might look for more conceptual skills—what Dan Schwarz calls *preparation for future learning* [278]. With my Emile students, I tested computer science knowledge by (for example) asking what happened in the computer when a user clicked on a button on the screen. That's a fairly technical detail. Maybe instead what's being learned are more fundamental computational ideas such as the following.

- Computers are powerful but limited. They don't have an intelligent being inside of them (as in Pea's superbug [244]).

- Programs are sequential and literal, with every line of the program being executed in sequence. We know that students tend to view programs as being a parallel process, a set of constraints or events [236].

- There are a handful of operations that computers can do. Understanding the primitive operations of the *notional machine* [77, 78, 297] is a key learning outcome of introductory computing courses. Computers can test data and make choices based on the result. Computers can iterate over actions forever until stopped or until a condition is met. But the first step to understanding the notional machine is to realize that there is one.

- We have to transform our problems to make them understandable to a computer. You can't just say, "And then the projectile falls." Rather, you have to figure out *how* the projectile falls, and in so describing that process, the physics and algebra learning can take place [282].

These are perfectly obvious to anyone who has programmed. We have evidence to lead us to believe that none of these is evident to students before they enter their first computer science class. Therefore, all of these ideas must be learned somewhere, and these ideas are common across programming situations. They will likely transfer.

There is little evidence to believe that students are learning higher-order thinking skills by learning programming. Computer science and programming are useful to support other learning. There are benefits even without expecting such significant transfer. Programming is a great medium for expression and for exploring causality [282], and that makes it a powerful medium for learning in many domains.

3.7 SUMMARY: SYNERGY BETWEEN COMPUTING AND OTHER DOMAINS

Learning programming can be synergistic. Seymour Papert made the argument long ago that programming can offer a medium for learning something like mathematics or science—more deeply than without programming [137]. There are still open research questions about how to create these synergies, how much of programming is needed to achieve those synergies, and what the design process is for these synergistic learning environments.

Learning programming is unlikely to result in these advantages without explicitly designing for these synergies. Just learning programming has not been shown to result in generalized problem-solving skills. Such skills are hard to teach. The examples in this chapter show that we can teach mathematics and science (and other subjects) with programming as the medium if we design for it.

I suggest that a learner-centered design process is a good start. An effective design respects the learner's desired learning goals. Authenticity of the activity is described in terms of the community of practice that the student wants to join. An effective design convinces the student that the effort spent in learning programming will result in success, as described by expectancy-value theory.

CHAPTER 4

Media Computation and Contextualized Computing Education

Some people learn computing for reasons other than the leverage it will provide to learn something else. Sometimes, people learn computing because they want to learn computing—and not because it will get them a great programming job. The faculty at Georgia Tech decided in the late 1990's that their students should know computing. They bought into the argument that it's an important skill in a technological society. They believed that it gave their students an advantage over students at schools who didn't make that commitment.

As of Fall 1999, every undergraduate student at Georgia Tech had to take a course in computer science that included programming [123]. The story of how we made that work provides insights into how to provide computing education at the undergraduate level that meet learners' needs and goals, even when those goals are not professional software development. Increasingly, non-computing undergraduate students need to learn about computing, but that requires a different approach from what we offer our computing undergraduate students.

4.1 TEACHING ONE COURSE FOR ALL

When we first started requiring computer science for all undergraduates, we offered only one course for everyone. We offered only a single introduction to Calculus, Biology, and Physics, therefore Computer Science seemed to call for a similar approach. There was a particular concern that creating a *majors* course and a *non-majors* course would create a two-tiered model. Computing faculty's attention and resources would go to the majors' tier, and the non-majors' tier would get little.

The course received considerable attention from the College of Computing. We used innovative curricular approaches, starting with Shackelford's pseudo-code approach to introductory computing [280] and later transitioning to the Scheme-based *How to Design Programs* curriculum [93]. We used innovative pedagogy including a large number of undergraduate teaching assistants and required one-on-one meetings between students and their near-peer TA's [37].

From 1999–2003, the average pass rate for the course was about 78%. From what we know about the pass rates for introductory computer science courses, that's pretty good. An international survey of introductory computer science courses found that most courses have pass rates between 50–70% [20]. Our 78% pass rate[1] seemed reasonable.

The story changed when we looked at individual majors. That 78% number reflected all students at Georgia Tech, which are primarily Engineering and Computing students. When we looked at individual majors in the Ivan Allen College of Liberal Arts, College of Architecture, and the College of Management,[2] we saw a very different story (Table 4.1). The pass rates were 50% or worse.

Table 4.1: Success rates for specific majors at Georgia Tech in the required introductory computer science course from Fall 1999 to Spring 2002

Architecture	46.70%
Biology	64.40%
Economics	53.50%
History	46.50%
Management	48.50%
Public Policy	47.90%

Those Engineering and Computing majors are mostly male at Georgia Tech. In Table 4.2, we see the total, male, and female pass rates for the last three semesters of the one-class-for-all solution. We see that the female pass rate is substantially lower than the male pass rate for two of the three semesters.

Table 4.2: Total, male, and female pass rates for last three semesters of the single required computing course at Georgia Tech

	Pass	Withdraw/Fail
Total Fall01	70.98%	29.02%
Females Fall01	59.55%	40.45%
Males Fall01	73.63%	26.37%
Total Sp02	65.03%	34.87%
Females Sp02	65.56%	34.44%
Males Sp02	64.81%	35.04%
Total Fall02	70.98%	29.02%
Females Fall02	59.55%	40.45%
Males Fall02	73.63%	26.37%

[1]We are defining *pass* as those who do not withdraw from the class or receive a D or an F (non-passing grades).
[2]Now the Scheller College of Business.

4.1.1   WHAT'S WRONG WITH ONE COURSE?

Around the same time that we were realizing that our one-course solution wasn't working at Georgia Tech, several studies came out describing the problems of computing education in the U.S. The most insightful of these was the Margolis and Fisher book, *Unlocking the Clubhouse*, which described how Carnegie Mellon University increased their percentage of female undergraduate students in their Computer Science majors to over 40% [204]. Other influential reports were *Tech Savvy* from the American Association of University Women (AAUW) [1], and *Preparing Women and Minorities for the IT Workforce* from the American Association for the Advancement of Science (AAAS).

When describing how students perceived the curriculum in computer science courses, these studies used words like "tedious," "boring," and "irrelevant." The activity of programming requires a lot of attention to detail, so "tedious" and "boring" are neither surprising nor incorrect. The label "irrelevant" seems surprising. In our technological society with ubiquitous computing, how could a class in *computer science* be *irrelevant*?

When we talked to students in the required course and asked them about their experiences, we got a clearer sense of how a course in computer science could be irrelevant. The examples and the homework didn't connect to what the students saw as being useful or relevant. Here are some interview exchanges [263].

Q: Is CS useful to you?

Student 1: I don't know yet. Some of the examples that we've done you can see how you can apply the concepts to real life. Like there was an example with seeing how when you make a deposit in the bank it finds the balance, you can see how that's related to real life, but I don't know if you can do that with Scheme.

Q: Is CS relevant to your career and/or personal life?

Student 3: Maybe, I'm not sure yet. I don't know about my personal life, but I guess if I want to be a doctor later, yeah, the skills I learned will be important, like logical thinking.

Student 1: I still don't know about how it will apply to my career. Personal? Right. Like, I just got back from lunch with (my friend),and he suggested that we could decide where to go to eat by making up lists of restaurants. Right. (Laughs)

We decided that we would attempt to engage students by creating new courses that wrapped a story around the course. We invented *contextualized computing education* [290] where we use an application area to design the class examples and all the assignments. Instead of having one computer science course that could meet the requirement, we created three.

- The existing one course would continue, and it would be taken by B.S. in CS majors and many majors from the College of Science.

- A second course was developed for the College of Engineering majors. David Smith wrote the textbook for that course [290]. He used the same sequencing and main topics of the HTDP book [93]. The language of the course was MATLAB, a popular programming language among Engineering professionals. The examples in the textbook were drawn from Engineering faculty around Georgia Tech who actually used MATLAB in their work.

- The third course, for Liberal Arts, Architecture, and Management/Business majors, was the one that I developed: *Introduction to Media Computation* [122].

4.2   THE DESIGN AND DEVELOPMENT OF MEDIA COMPUTATION

Andrea Forte documented the design process we used in developing the Media Computation course [102, 135]. We started with the learning objectives for the course: Georgia Tech's requirements for the course and external recommendations (like the *ACM/IEEE 2001 Computing Curriculum*) [264, 265]. The course was owned by the faculty of Georgia Tech, and we needed to meet their goals. We added goals recommended by external reports like Margolis & Fisher and the AAUW report.

- Students need to see the course as *relevant*.

- Students should find *opportunities for creativity* in the course. We knew that female computer science students reported being surprised by how much opportunity for creativity there was in CS [329]. We wanted to highlight the opportunity for creativity to make the class more engaging.

- Students should see *computing as a social experience*. The stereotype of computer science as being asocial has negatively influenced retention [204].

We made an explicit effort to minimize how much programming we asked students to learn. Our goal was for students to learn the core of programming in Python (e.g, assignment, for loops, conditionals, defining functions, manipulating lists), and to learn it well, so that it would likely transfer to new languages. There is much more that we would like these students to know about computer science. We chose to help them learn *generative* knowledge that would grow and could be applied to other domains, and for them to leave the class motivated to use that knowledge and gain more.

We chose the context of manipulation of media based on learning objectives and on the majors of the learners in our course. For these majors, the computer is less a tool of calculation than of communication. They use the computer to produce Powerpoint and Keynote slides, to manipulate images in Photoshop and Gimp, and to edit video in iMovie and Final Cut Pro.

We found that we could address all our computing learning objectives using the Media Computation context. Here are a few examples.

- In every introductory computing course, we ask students to do something to every piece of data in a collection, like computing the average of all the test scores in an array or list. We achieve the same goals in Media Computation by having students iterate across all the pixels in a picture[3] to compute a negative or grayscale image, or to find the largest sample in a sound so that the volume can be increased without distortion.[4]

- In every introductory computing course, we use conditionals to process just some data in a collection. We do the same thing in Media Computation by removing red eye without changing any red in the person's outfit.

- In every introductory computing course, we talk about algorithms that work the same across any kinds of data. The process for scaling up or down a picture is essentially the same as the one in which we shift a sound up or down in frequency.

We chose to emphasize to the students that the Media Computation course would:

- Help them to understand better the applications that they use already. The Media Computation course as a computer *science* class would be like other sciences. It would help them to understand the world in which they live.

- Give them a superpower to manipulate media beyond any application. Students told us how hard it was to figure out how to apply a *particular* effect in Photoshop. With Media Computation, you always had the option to write the code to do what you wanted.

Because we were using a learner-centered design process, we created a *feedback process* by which we would check our design decisions with our learners and their teachers. We created Web surveys and asked teachers of freshman classes (e.g., English composition, Calculus, and Biology) to invite their students to answer. These were mechanisms for gathering impressions and attitudes, and for bouncing ideas off of students. As we had examples to show, we invited non-CS majors who were then enrolled in our introductory computing course to pizza lunches where we presented the class and got feedback on the plans.

We set up an advisory board of faculty from across campus to tell us what they thought about the class. Some of the advice was about content. For example, faculty in Architecture wanted to make sure that we talked about the difference between extending a line in Photoshop (at the pixel level) and extending a line in a design tool like AutoCAD (which involves changing an underlying structural representation). Engaging the faculty as advisors was important.

- Our goal was to be learner-centered. The faculty from those other departments had insights about teaching these non-CS majors that CS faculty would not.

---

[3]Digital pictures are composed of *pixels*, several thousand in each dimension. Each pixel has a color associated with it, made up of red, green, and blue components.
[4]Digital sounds are made up of *samples* which are measures of air pressure on the microphone. There are 44,100 samples per second in CD-quality sound.

- After creating the course, we had to convince the non-CS programs to adopt it. Our advisors could inform their departments about the course, and be able to explain the course in terms that addressed those departments' needs and concerns.

The choice of the programming language and other infrastructure elements of the course came late in the process. We made the decision with our student informants and faculty advisors. Our original plan was to use Scheme, since that was already being used in the introductory course, but both students and faculty rejected that. Students saw Scheme as "more of the same." One faculty advisor cornered me at a meeting and asked, "I heard about your new course. You're not going to use Scheme, are you? You know, that's what they use at MIT. That's not appropriate for my students, you know?" We proposed both Java and Squeak. Java was branded by the non-CS faculty as too technical, since it was used in our upper-level courses for CS majors. Squeak was simply too unknown to be vetted [119, 120].

In the end, we chose Python. Python was easily vetted by the faculty with a few web searches. It's generally perceived to be easily adopted. Faculty found it comforting that companies used Python, so it had a level of *authenticity* to it. Students liked the kinds of programs we could write with it. A simple function to decrease the red in a picture looked like this:

```
def decreaseRed(picture):
   for pixel in getPixels(picture):
      value=getRed(pixel)
      setRed(pixel,value * 0.5)
```

This function `decreaseRed` accepts a picture as input, so it works on any image that the student uses. The variable `pixel` will represent all the pixels (`getPixels(picture)`) of the picture, one at a time. For each pixel, our function pulls out the amount of redness in that pixel, then decreases it by 50% and puts it back as the redness for that pixel.

4.2.1 SCAFFOLDING IN MEDIA COMPUTATION

The actual implementation of the course involved creating a scaffolded programming environment and scaffolded curriculum (as was described in the last chapter in the discussion of Emile). We created supports to promote student success (that might not have happened otherwise). We expected the scaffolding to fade (go away).

Traditional Python did not have all the cross-platform multimedia libraries that we needed. We implemented the course using Jython (Python implemented in Java) and built the libraries we needed in Java. It was much easier to create the cross-platform multimedia libraries we needed in Java than in C. There was no programming environment for students in Jython, so we created the Jython Environment for Students (JES).

All the media computation supports we created (to manipulate pictures, sounds, and video) were not part of Python or Jython. We implemented these functions (like `makePicture` and `getPixels`), classes, and methods in external libraries. To access these libraries, the students' programs needed to start with the line `from media import *`. But we didn't want to students to have to know that on the first day of class. Instead, we modified JES so that the `import` statement would be invisibly added to the start of the program. That's an example of a scaffold. By the end of the course, students were using a variety of libraries with different kinds of `import` statements, and we explained how to import the media library to use it in Jython without JES. We did not want concepts of libraries and `import` to be additional complexity and cognitive load (i.e., something else to be kept in mind which might not be germane to the immediate learning goal) on the first day of the course.

We wrote a textbook for the Python version of the course. The sequence of topics in the curriculum was different than in most Python textbooks. This was a kind of curricular scaffolding.

- We started teaching the `for` loop as seen previously, `for pixel in getPixels(picture)`. When we start with sounds, we introduced `for sample in getSamples(sound)`. In most languages, a `for` loop is used to iterate through a set of numbers (e.g., `for num in range(0,10)`), or all the indices for a set (e.g., `for index in range(len(elements))`). The Python `for` loop is actually a kind of `for-each` loop. We introduced the `for` loop so that it could be read "for each pixel in the pixels of the picture" and "for each sample in the samples of the sound." Studies in the 1970's found that non-programmers understood *operations on a set* more easily than *iteration* [217]. The curriculum does reach the use of `for` loops for indices, but that's not where we started.

- We chose to put off teaching the `else` clause of a conditional (`if`) statement. Most textbooks teach `else` as soon as the `if` statement is introduced. Significant empirical evidence suggests that the `else` clause is unnatural and difficult for novices [113]. In studies of non-programmers being asked to write out how they think programs are specified, an `else` clause is simply not invented by non-programmers [217, 236]. In studies of novice programmers contrasting explicit `if` statements (e.g., `if P...end P; if not P...end not P;`) to the same code with `else` clauses, novice programmers are able to read the non-`else` versions of the code *ten times* faster and with fewer errors than the `else` versions of the same code [113]. Belief that `else` is *easy* is an example of an expert's blind spot—experts don't recall how they thought as novices, and they trust their content knowledge (i.e., that `else` is common and easy) over their pedagogical content knowledge (introduced in Chapter 1) [221].

The supports we created for the course have continued to be used for over a decade now. JES and the related libraries are still used today, with dozens of contributing authors. Since the libraries were already in Java, we were able to create a Java version of the course with little additional technical development [131].

4.2.2   OFFERING THE FIRST MEDIA COMPUTATION COURSES

The Media Computation course was structured around projects that would provide students with the opportunity to express their creativity. For example, we wanted students to be able to build *image collages* where the same image would be composed several times into a larger canvas (Figure 4.1). The image would be copied as-is once, and then at least a couple other times making any modifications that the students wanted: changing colors, resizing, cropping, reversing, etc. Then the whole canvas would have to be mirrored horizontally or vertically, to create a nice spatial layout. Key to this assignment is that students could use any images they wanted. We cared about students being able to specify the process of how the collage was constructed (i.e., the program that they wrote), but the choice of images and how they were manipulated could be left to the student. The assignments leading up to the collage assignment were all about preparing students to do that.

Figure 4.1: Example collages by Media Computation students.

The open-ended, creative nature of the Media Computation assignments motivated the students. We saw that in our study results [102, 126], and I saw it as the teacher. Students would often write over a hundred lines of code for the collage assignment. I once taught the course in a study abroad setting. The course was just me and a couple dozen students meeting daily for 90 minutes, so I got more insight into the students' process than I do in the normal 150-student lecture on-campus. Students would come to my office hours daily to show me what they were doing and ask for help. Sometimes they would just plop down next to me and start working. "Do you have any questions?" I'd ask. "No, but I'll work here, so when I do, you'll be right there." Students would often show me their collages and ask for help. "Looks like you have all the pieces there," I'd say. "Yeah, but it's *not* the way *I* want it to look yet!" Students would push themselves *beyond* the requirements of the assignment when they wanted to realize their own creative vision.

Students saw the *relevance* of Media Computation. Andrea Forte led a team of researchers to study the first Media Computation courses [101–103, 135]. She used surveys and interviews to get a sense of what was going on in the course. The common message was about relevance and value.

> "It made me understand more how computers work so I can use them better. Helped me use the normal programs like email and internet better. And I know how picture editing works, which is cool."

We used an early Wiki designed for students in the course as a *Homework Gallery*. Students were encouraged to share their products on the *CoWeb* (Collaborative Website). Students told us that this changed the course into a social activity.

Q: What do you think about the homework galleries on the CoWeb?

Student 4: It's nice to see other people, like what they did with it… And there is no better feeling than getting something done and knowing that you've done it right. Like the soapbox[5] sometimes is just like "I did it!" and posting to the CoWeb just adds onto that.

Student 3: I don't ever look at it [the homework gallery] until after I'm done. I have a thing about not wanting to copy someone else's ideas. I just wish I had more time to play around with that and make neat effects. But JES will be on my computer forever, so… the nice thing about this class is that you could go as deep into the homework as you wanted. So, I'd turn it [the collage] in, and then me and my roommate would do more after to see what we could do with it.

We have evidence that students clearly saw the course as relevant. However, it wasn't actually *authentic* in terms of reflecting a community of practice. Shaffer and Resnick developed a definition of authenticity that had several factors [281]. Authentic learning featured:

- authentic activities aligned with the world outside of school, e.g., students perceive that the learning activities are aligned with an external community of practice;

- topics aligned with what learners want to know, e.g., students perceive the value of the content being taught;

- assessment aligned with instruction which is aligned with practice, e.g., the assessment measures what was taught, and that is what is used in practice; and

- methods of inquiry aligned with the discipline, e.g., students are learning to think in the ways of a community of practice.

---

[5]A space for comments that would appear at the top of every CoWeb page

For students in Liberal Arts, Architecture, and Business, it's challenging to be authentic in the Shaffer and Resnick model. There isn't an easily identified community of practice of programming with media in these disciplines. The practice in Media Computation isn't even what real media programmers use. Professional programmers who build photo filters or audio manipulations don't use Python to iterate over individual pixels and samples.

We constructed a sense of authenticity for the course [136]. We worked at convincing the students that this knowledge had value and "counted" (in the sense of being accountable disciplinary knowledge [304]). In the class, we talk about how chromakey[6] is used in television and movies, before we talk about the algorithm. We worked hard to make sure that the textbook, the programming environment, the examples in class, and all the assignments were aligned, e.g., used the same terms and referenced the same algorithms. The TA's in the course often did the assignments, too, then shared their output in the homework galleries, so that there was a sense of more established people in the community of practice engaging in the same practices. As behavioral economists have found [165], the consistency of the story is more critical to believability than its completeness or correctness.

The class worked because it created a willing suspension of disbelief about its authenticity. It didn't necessarily convince students that they wanted to be part of a professional software developer community of practice, but students did see it as relevant. Students told us in several studies that they found that the course informed their daily lives [263, 314]. One student told us in a survey:

> Other than making me a little more aware about what I can make the computer do, it hasn't changed the way I particularly interact with technology. Yet I am uninterested in this field. However, I now have a *MUCH* better understanding of the people who are interested in this field, how they view things, and how to interact with them more easily. For this, I appreciate the CS class greatly.

4.3   IMPACT OF MEDIA COMPUTATION

We can discuss two sets of results about the impact of Media Computation and the contextualized computing education approach to teaching computing. The first is within Georgia Tech. The second is what we saw at other institutions, which support the claim that contextualized computing education is generally valuable—not just at my institution.

4.3.1   IMPACT WITHIN GEORGIA TECH

The Media Computation class had an immediate impact on retention in that introductory course. Table 4.3 shows the success rates in Media Computation compared with those same majors (Table 4.1) who had low success rates.

---

[6]The "green screen" effect where a background color is swapped for another image to create the illusion that a foreground character is in a different background.

Table 4.3: Change in success rates from before Media Computation (Fall 1999 to Spring 2002) to after (from Spring 2003 to Fall 2005)

	Success Rate Pre-MediaComp	Success Rate With MediaComp
Architecture	46.70%	85.70%
Biology	64.40%	90.40%
Economics	53.50%	92.00%
History	46.50%	67.60%
Management	48.50%	87.80%
Public Policy	47.90%	85.40%

Table 4.4: Pass and Withdraw/Fail Rates in first three semesters of Media Computation

	Pass	Withdraw/Fail
Total Fall03	86%	13%
Females Fall03	88%	10%
Males Fall03	85%	15%
Total Sp04	90%	9%
Females Sp04	92%	8%
Males Sp04	88%	11%
Total Fall04	80%	20%
Females Fall04	83%	17%
Males Fall04	77%	23%

When we look at the first three semesters of Media Computation (Table 4.4), in comparison with the last three semesters of the all-in-one course (Table 4.2), we see a marked improvement in pass rates. In particular, we see that women are doing better than men in some semesters. In 2013, I wrote a retrospective paper about the first ten years of Media Computation, and we looked up the pass rates for the course. Over ten years, the pass rate consistently stayed better than 85% [126].

One way in which the course was relevant for these students is that they actually *used* it. About a year after we started teaching Media Computation, we did a survey of all the students who took the course in the first two semesters. Over a quarter (27%) of the respondents had manipulated new media since leaving the class. 19% of the respondents had actually written programs since class had ended, even without taking more computer science. That's a notable indication of application of computing knowledge by non-professional programmers. Even those who didn't program, told us about how the class changed their experience of computing.

"I have learned more about the big picture behind computer science and programming. This has helped me to figure out how to use programs that I've never used before, troubleshoot problems on my own computer, use programs that I was already familiar with in a more sophisticated way, and given me more confidence to try to problem solve, explore, and fix my computer."

"Definitely makes me think of what is going on behind the scenes of such programs like Photoshop and Illustrator."

4.3.2   IMPACT OUTSIDE GEORGIA TECH

Gainesville College in northern Georgia was the first place to adopt Media Computation after Georgia Tech [314]. They similarly saw a rise in their pass rates. Their pass rates were 70.2% across 2000–2003. They rose to 77.8% in the first Summer semester that they adopted Media Computation and 84.6% in the first full Fall semester class.

The next published study of use of Media Computation was at University of Illinois—Chicago (UIC). UIC is a more diverse school than Georgia Tech or Gainesville [289], so it provided a chance to see if the approach might work to engage a broader population of students. They adopted Media Computation in their introductory course for CS majors. Their success rate with their old course was 75.9%, which rose to 84.1% with Media Computation.

The biggest study of Media Computation was at the University of California, San Diego (UCSD) [288]. They changed their introductory course to use Media Computation (in Java) as the curriculum, then combined it with research-based pedagogy. They used Peer Instruction to engage students in lecture, and Pair Programming to encourage social and collaborative learning when working on homework [253]. Over several years, they saw a dramatic rise in their retention. They improved their retention of CS majors into their sophomore year—from 51% of majors retained into the second year before the intervention, up to 81% retained in the second year after [254]. UCSD is on the quarter system. Changing one ten-week (quarter long) class had measurable impacts a year later.

Media Computation influenced other curricular efforts. Cynthia Bailey Lee created a Media Computation class using MATLAB [183]. Sam Rebelsky created a class using LISP that was influenced by Media Computation [259]. Brad Miller and David Ranum created a Python textbook that drew on several different contexts, with image manipulation as one of those [215]. The Institute for Personal Robotics in Education (IPRE) built their Python libraries to include similar Media Computation functions so that students could do processing on the camera images taken by the student-programmed robots [10, 305]. A processing-based introductory computing course was influenced by the curriculum and design of Media Computation [114].

4.3.3   WHY DOES MEDIA COMPUTATION WORK, AND WHERE DOESN'T IT?

The key idea behind Media Computation is *contextualized computing education* [124]. If the learner perceives the *relevance* of the course context, the course is more concrete and less abstract. There is increased motivation to succeed. That motivation increases success rates.

Andrea Forte did a careful study where she looked at the success rates in both the Media Computation class and in the Engineering MATLAB course [103]. She found that the Engineering students also saw the relevance in their course. *Both* classes had a rise in success rates. Media Computation is an instance of a more general lesson that was also true for the Engineering class.

The importance of the design goals that underlie Media Computation has been supported by later work. Lecia Barker conducted a survey of over 2,000 computing students from 14 institutions and found that relevant, meaningful assignments was the most important factor in retaining students [13], even more than the second biggest predictor, student-faculty interaction. Students leave computer science in part because they believe that it is an "asocial, coding-only field with little connection to the outside world" [25]. A report from Google based on a survey of 1000 women and 600 men found that females who were unfamiliar with computer science described it "boring, hard, and difficult" (three of the top five terms associated), but those familiar with computer science saw it as "creative." Social encouragement was the most critical factor in getting those women to pursue more computer science [111].

We did think that we might get more students to study computer science when we first built Media Computation. It didn't happen [126] and Mike Hewner conducted a study to figure out why [140]. He asked students in 2007, four years after we started the Media Computation and Engineering classes, to tell him their stories about using computing. He wanted to understand the impact of a contextualized introductory course through the rest of the students' undergraduate career. He found that the introductory course had little impact in terms of change in student attitudes toward continuing in computing as a field or a career. If a student was pursuing a major (say, in computing or engineering) in which she expected to use computing, then the introductory course gave useful preparation for that major, and the student enjoyed the course. If a student was pursuing a major in which she expected to use little computing, then the introductory course was a required course, and it was typically followed by little computing in the other courses in that major. The course may have been fun, and even useful in terms of understanding computing in their lives, but not life-changing.

In Lave and Wenger terms, the students had a community of practice that they wanted to join. If the introductory course supported that path, then it was great. If it didn't, then the course might still be relevant to their lives, but not to their careers.

If we think about it in terms of Eccles' model of academic achievement, we see that we have changed the utility of the course. We haven't changed students perceptions of computer science or whether they fit into computer science. We haven't changed the community of practice that they want to join. Instead, we made the course more valuable for what the learners wanted, e.g., to know about the technology and media in their lives. That was the outcome for which we designed.

4.4   A SECOND COURSE IN MEDIA COMPUTATION

When more than 80% of all the liberal arts, architecture, and business students who took our introductory course *succeeded*, we discovered that some students wanted a *second* course. Recall that one of the differences between designing for learners and experts is that learners can be expected to change. As students learn, they are more likely to change their identity [144], especially as they gain in literacy. It's not surprising, then, that students who engage with computing might decide to develop their literacy and develop an identity as computationally literate.

In the first few semesters of teaching Media Computation [314] at Georgia Tech we asked students two questions on surveys.

- "I would like to take more courses in Computer Science." Over 50% of the Georgia Tech students disagreed or strongly disagreed with that statement. Only 23% agreed or strongly agreed. (The rest were neutral.)

- "I would like to take more courses in Media Computation." 42.1% agreed or strongly agreed with that statement, with 34% disagreeing or strongly disagreeing.

We took those results to say that those students who wanted a second course wanted it to use a media computation context. Again, we looked at Georgia Tech's computing requirements and the ACM/IEEE Computing Curricula to help us determine learning objectives [264, 265]. We decided to teach Java, so that students would be able to move into Georgia Tech's computer science sequence of classes for CS majors, if they wanted to go beyond the second course. We decided to teach core data structures, as a natural second course in the ACM/IEEE sequence.

We chose a *driving question* for the Media Computation data structures class. A driving question is useful in project-based learning to direct student inquiry, design, and construction [27, 177]. Our driving question was, "How did the wildebeests stampede in Disney's *The Lion King*?" The scene where the wildebeests stampede in *The Lion King* was notable as being the first where Disney animators didn't draw their characters. All the wildebeests were modeled and then simulated [69]. To explain how that worked, we needed to explain to students linked lists, networks, stacks, and queues. The target assignments involved building and using these data structures to model musical sequences, scenes, character movement, and predator-prey simulations.

The goals were different for this second course. We weren't worried about retention anymore. Nobody was required to take this course. We still wanted to students to see *relevance* for the course. We were also interested in whether the driving question worked. Unlike the general theme of "media computation," the second course had a *narrative*. Did the students see that all the parts of the class added up to an answer to how the wildebeests charged over the ridge?

Lana Yarosh conducted an innovative study to explore the questions of relevance and narrative [330]. In a single semester, she ran three mini-studies.

- She surveyed the class to understand what they were interested in and why they were taking the course.

- Over several weeks, she had half-hour interviews with several students about how the class was going. She analyzed these interviews to come up with statements about the course that were true for the interviewees.

- At the final exam, she had students take a second survey where she asked the whole class to agree or disagree with the statements that came from the interviewees.

One of the clear outcomes was that the media context did not work for all the students anymore. One interviewee said, "I don't need to make pretty pictures. I need to be able to perform calculations." That quote became the survey prompt "Working with media makes this class less useful to me." 11% of the class agreed or strongly agreed with this statement. 70% of the class agreed or strongly agreed that working with the media made the class *more interesting*.

The media context was *less* relevant in this second course for about 11% of the class. As one interviewee put it:

But in terms of interest, I think some of the stuff we're doing is very interesting. I think working with these different pictures and things—maybe that's why we do it. I think for me maybe it sacrifices a little relevancy and makes up for it in interesting material.

When asked whether they viewed time working with media as time they would rather spend learning the material in greater depth, the majority of students disagreed or strongly disagreed (59%). The context of the course served to motivate the students so that they became engaged in the material *without* finding it directly relevant.

Students perceived the narrative that pervaded the class and were willing to suspend their disbelief and become engaged in the material. They saw the narrative. One interviewee said "You could see the progress made from the beginning of the class." The final project was "just neat to put it all together." A third student commented that the final project that involved simulations with characters was "the goal of the course." The narrative played an important role in student motivation, as one interviewee put it: "I felt like that tied everything together, so that was pretty neat."

The constructed narrative of the Media Computation data structures class worked to motivate the class. But students were more savvy in the second course. Not all the students saw it as quite so relevant.

4.5 DESIGN OF A COMPUTING COURSE FOR NON-COMPUTER SCIENCE MAJORS

The Media Computation classes serve as examples of how to use a learner-centered design approach as a starting point for the design of a computing course for non-computing majors.

1. **Figure out what has to be learned**. For students in an undergraduate program, a lot of what has to be learned has been decided by course objectives, by the faculty community, and by other stakeholders. As we'll see in the next chapter, sometimes the students tell you what they need to learn.

2. **Understand the learner's motivations and goals**. We made a significant effort with both classes to use surveys and interviews to understand what motivated our students. What was the community of practice that they were motivated by? What do they want to learn? What do they know? What are they interested in?

3. **Find a context in which you can teach #1 respecting #2**. Media as a context worked because it allowed us to address our learning goals within the motivations and goals of our students.

4. **Assess the results**. The design of a course involves making hypotheses. We thought that we would improve retention with our new first course, and that worked. We thought that media would be perceived as a relevant context for students in both classes. It was, but less so in the second class. We needed to test our hypotheses, to see if our designs worked.

These may seem obvious, but these are not common practice. In Chapter 6, I argue that computing teachers too often aim to filter out students who "don't belong" rather than change teaching to meet student needs. In Chapter 7, I propose changes in how we teach computing at the undergraduate level to make it more successful with non-computing students.

There is a clear need for more learner-centered computing courses for people who are *not* going to be professional software developers. For example, the Software Carpentry effort helps scientists and engineers to develop the computational skills they need [324]. As Scaffidi, Shaw, and Myers tells us, many people will need to develop computing skills for their success [274]. However, many of them will realize this late—when they are working adult professionals, after coursework. The next chapter addresses how we might reach those students.

CHAPTER 5

Adults as Computing Learners

The learner-centered design model presented in the first chapter was updated by later work. Chris Quintana and Elliot Soloway developed a more elaborated learner-centered design framework [257, 258, 296]. For example, their model recommends starting the learner-centered design process from what the students find challenging. The original model didn't address the *process* of design. The Quintana and Soloway design methods help us understand how to apply learner-centered design to computing education.

Quintana and Soloway's framework is meant to be used in designing educational software, but still offers useful insights when designing computing education. They used their framework to develop handheld tools for science education and sophisticated tools to guide students in computational science [198, 199]. In their model, they describe the difference between (expert) users and learners like this:

> Learners do not possess the same domain expertise as users. They share neither an understanding of a work domain nor the tasks within it with their professional counterparts.

Learner-centered design is different when our learners are working professionals. These are adults who are outside the classroom and who have enormous expertise, and now want to learn something new. Based on what we know about end-user programmers, they probably want to learn something new that helps them with their current professions [220]. We can still use a learner-centered design perspective as a starting place to develop learning opportunities for these adult students. We still consider who they are, what they want to learn, and how their expertise differs from professional software developers.

Adults differ from Quintana and Soloway's learners in several ways:

- They know *their* work domain very well. They don't know the computer science work domain. They may not want to.

- They have a professional identity. Sometimes that identity is in conflict with learning computer science.

- They have a purpose for learning computing, which usually has nothing to do with becoming a professional software developer.

- They are time poor. As adults and working professionals, they do not have the luxury of learning in the classroom, even if they would be willing to do that. They need learning opportunities that fit into their lives and practice.

In this chapter, I present two stories of adults as computing learners. They differ in important ways. Graphic designers who learn to code reject becoming computer scientists or programmers. High school teachers want to learn computer science to teach their students, but they themselves don't have any purpose to code. The approaches to teaching each of these groups differ because the learning goals differ.

5.1   GRAPHIC AND WEB DESIGNERS AS END-USER PROGRAMMERS

Web designers are a class of end-users who find themselves thinking about the code underlying the websites that they design. These are people who think about the layout, but who do not deal with the databases and Javascript programming that form the infrastructure of websites. When asked to think about them, they are often at a loss. The way that they think about the Web doesn't match the way that the Web actually works. In a study by Rode, Rosson, and Pérez-Quiñones, web designers were faced with questions like "What do you think the web site must do to keep track of the fact that you are logged in even though you go from page to page?" They did not have an idea of how it happened. They thought of it in terms of surface features [267], as novices (e.g., in physics) will [181]. Rode et al. tell us that one participant described the status of *being logged in*: "…is the status quo, it's like an on/off thing, a toggle type of situation." They can imagine being logged in as a kind of a radio button, but don't know how it might be implemented.

When these web designers decide to learn something about programming, they don't start out looking for classes in computer science. Rosson et al. surveyed over 300 web developers [271] and determined that they rely on online resources. Rather than classes, they prefer pages with frequently asked questions (FAQs), books, and shared code from peers.

Most web designers work in terms of tools, like Dreamweaver. If they deal with the specification of web pages, in terms of HTML and CSS, they face some of the same problems that novice programmers do. Thomas Park studied how people learn HTML and CSS, and the mistakes that they make when doing it [240, 241]. HTML and CSS are structured much like a programming language, with delimiters, a hierarchical structure, and clear errors, e.g., creating items for lists without first creating a list. The pickiness of a formal notation that is interpreted by a machine, not by a human who might be able to predict what you meant to say, is a challenge for someone who focuses on how things look and not how they work.

5.1.1   HELPING GRAPHIC DESIGNERS

Graphic designers and web designers have a significant overlap. Brian Dorn started his research by looking at the graphic designers who came to programming in a slightly different way. Rather than wanting to dig into the mechanisms of the web pages that they were designing, Dorn's end-user programmers wanted to save time (over 80% gave that reason [72]). Graphic design tools like Photoshop and GIMP are scriptable. It's possible to write a program to do something quickly and over many pictures, which might be tedious and take a long time by hand. Many of the graphic designers that Brian studied were freelance consultants. Time was money. If they could save time by automating something, it saved them money.

Like Rosson's survey of web designers, Dorn's graphic designers relied almost entirely on on-line resources. They made heavy use of code repositories, where peer graphic designers and others (e.g., Adobe, the company that produces Photoshop) leave cool and useful examples for others. Web designers often grab a piece of code from the repository, study it, then modify it for their own purposes.

One disadvantage of this source of learning is that you can only learn from what's there. Dorn and Tew studied programs in one of these code repositories [75]. 30% of the code used no user-defined functions—it was just a long list of statements. Only 20% used objects. Only a third used `while` loops or nested loops.

Graphic designers see themselves as artists, not programmers. Dorn surveyed graphic designers who scripted. Over 70% had their formal training in art, photography, or other media. Over 80% said that they didn't see themselves as programmers. Yet all of them had written significant programs. One respondent said that he programmed to "build database-populated pages for print and CD catalog distribution."

The real challenge in helping this population learn programming is that they don't even *like* computer science or programmers. Dorn conducted an interview study with 12 graphic designers who program [73]. There were five women and seven men (because graphic designers who program are more gender-balanced than computer scientists), all adults. They don't see much use for computer science classes.

> P10: "I think that an academic study would make me a better programmer, but not by a whole lot."

They feel rejected by the programming community, and they reject programmers.

> P9: "I met a guy who programs ATM machines, and he busted me for calling myself a coder. He says, well no, you're a scripter. And the coders you know, they're down there in the dirty behind the scenes playing with the rendering buffers and you know, moving bits of memory back and forth."

> P2: "I went to a meeting for some kind of programmers, something or other. And they were *old*, and they were nerdy, and they were boring! And I'm like, this is not my personality. Like I can't work with people like that."

They don't reject programming. They feel empowered by it.

P12: "I don't like to code. But the things that the code can do is amazing, like you can come up with this and voila, you know, it's there…Because I mean like the code is just, there's so much you can do with code and stuff. It's just like wow "

It's not a surprise, then, that the graphic designers that Dorn surveyed and interviewed are not using computer science classes to help them learn programming. In terms of Lave and Wenger, the graphic designers do not see programmers at the center of their community of practice. They do not see themselves as programmers. Their academic background is in art and media, not computer science. They don't see much value in academic study of programming. The graphic designers have an identity that they see at odds with the identity of a programmer.

5.1.2   STARTING FROM THE LEARNING CHALLENGES

If we were going to help these graphic designers learn about computing, Quintana and Soloway would tell us to start from their challenges. What don't they know? What gets in the way of the graphic designers being successful at programming?

Dorn interviewed graphic designers to characterize their knowledge of computer science and programming [74]. He observed graphic designers working at tweaking program code like the kind that they might download from a repository. He found evidence that they *needed* some of that academic computer science that they were rejecting.

- Dorn observed graphic designers using web searches to find more information on the programs that they're modifying. Because they don't have traditional computer science knowledge, their searches aren't always productive. They might search for `JavaScript foo` (where `foo` is a variable in the program), not realizing that `foo` is just an arbitrary name and not a special library function. They search for the command `try`, not knowing that the technical term for what they're searching for is "*exception handling.*"

- Dorn observed graphic designers finding information that wasn't useful to them, but they didn't realize it because of their lack of knowledge. In an observation study, one of his end-user programmers spent a half hour reading a web page before Dorn informed the graphic designer, "That's a page on Java. You're programming in JavaScript. That page isn't relevant for you."

Dorn's graphic designers lacked basic computer science knowledge, e.g., that there were different programming languages, the terms used in the field, and the difference between arbitrary programmer-defined names and language-defined names. How do you provide computer science knowledge, that is actually needed, to end-user programmers who reject computer science? Dorn decided to build his intervention on top of his learners' existing practice. He knew that they already searched code repositories for useful programs. He decided to embed the information that they *needed* in the information that they *wanted*.

He created two different code resources [71, 76].

- The first one was a *code repository*, with the same features as code repositories that he already found on the Web [75]. For example, his repository had indices so that program code could be found in terms of code features or in terms of what Photoshop features it used.

- The second was a *case library*, with the exact same programs as in the code repository [71]. The difference was that each program in the case library included a story about *how* the code was written, and that story used the *computer science terms* for the program elements, e.g., "That's called a *boolean* variable."

He asked graphic designer-programmers to use one of his two resources. Both groups were given a set of programming challenges that were like the ones that graphic designers might naturally face. After the challenges, Dorn asked each group of users if they liked their resource. He gave them a small test about computer science—testing exactly the things that he had earlier learned that his learners did *not* typically learn.

- Each group *liked* the code resource they received. That's important because graphic designers are adults who *choose* what resources they use. If they don't like a resource, they won't use it—even if it's good for them.

- Each group was equally successful at the challenges Dorn posed them. Again, that's important because graphic designers will only choose to use a resource that actually helps them.

- The case library group learned new computer science terms that the code repository group did not learn.

The story of the graphic designer-programmers offers an approach to providing computing education to working adults. Dorn embedded computing education in the work practices and materials of the graphic designers. Adults may not be able to fit a class into their lives. Like our graphic designers, they may cringe at taking a course in "computer science" or "programming." We can, instead, provide the educational opportunities where they are already looking for information. Experts in human-centered computing sometimes refer to *information ecologies* [52], where those seeking information are *foraging* and *harvesting* the information they need. In this metaphor, Dorn fortified the information that was already being harvested with the nutrients that the foragers needed.

5.2 THE NEEDS OF COMPUTING TEACHERS AS COMPUTING LEARNERS

My second story of adults learning computing is about developing high school computer science teachers. Unlike mathematics, science, reading, or any other kind of high school teacher, there are few colleges or universities in the U.S. where a new teacher can learn to be a computer science teacher [180]. Other countries (notably, Israel and Germany) do have *pre-service* programs to develop new computer science teachers [108]. In the U.S., almost all new high school CS teachers learn *in-service*, i.e., while they're teaching something else in schools. That creates unique learning challenges.

In most U.S. states, computer science is classified as a *Career and Technical Education (CTE)* subject [180]. CTE teachers most commonly have a license or certificate to teach *business classes*. (Few U.S. states offer a certification to teach computer science.) The implication is that the teachers who are typically teaching computer science in the U.S. have not necessarily had much mathematics or science coursework, and very few have had any computer science courses. They are most often teaching classes in keyboarding, office applications, or web design.

There are surprisingly few well-prepared computer science teachers in the U.S. Depending on how you count, there are between 25,000–30,000 high schools in the U.S. There are roughly 2300 teachers of Advanced Placement Computer Science (Level A) in the U.S. Less than 10% of high schools in the U.S. have an AP CS teacher [87].

The problem is not unique to the U.S. The UK, Denmark, and New Zealand (among others) are facing the challenge of developing enough computer science teachers to provide access to computing education for all students [18, 31, 42]. The U.S. National Science Foundation (NSF) has set a goal of *CS10K*, having 10,000 well-prepared computer science teachers in 10,000 U.S. high schools [7]. It's a big challenge.

We have too few computer science teachers to meet the goals described in Chapter 1. Producing enough teachers is the bottleneck in increasing access to computing education [128]. Few teachers want to become CS teachers, as is described below. We have to smooth the way.

5.2.1   ADULTS LEARNING COMPUTER SCIENCE ONLINE

Our research group at Georgia Tech has over a decade of experience offering CS learning opportunities to high school teachers through Barbara Ericson's work in the *Institute for Computing Education at Georgia Tech* [88, 89, 132]. We are exploring how to provide CS learning opportunities to high school teachers *online* [91]. Quintupling the number of high school computer science teachers in the United States is going to be difficult and expensive. We will be hard-pressed to get 8000 new CS teachers into physical classrooms for enough time to learn all the content that they'll need—even without considering who teaches their classes while they're learning. There are models where teachers do some learning in classes in summer, then learn more online [112]. There are other models where teachers learn in their own classes with IT professionals teaching the content [147].

In most of these models, there is some online learning component. Taking a Quintana and Soloway perspective, we wondered what the challenges were for working professionals learning computer science online. Klara Benda did an interview study (with Amy Bruckman and me) of adults taking courses in an online Masters degree program at a university in Georgia [19].

Benda titled her paper, *When Life and Learning Do Not Fit: Challenges of Workload and Communication in Introductory Computer Science Online*, which gives away the punchline. The classes

Benda studied were taught using the pedagogy of a typical computer science course emphasizing an apprenticeship perspective. (Recall the *Teaching Perspectives Inventory* from Chapter 1.) There would be some kind of expository material (e.g., a lecture as a Powerpoint slide show or video to watch), then assignments in which students were meant to spend hours making sense of the lecture.

Benda's informants said that they could handle the content, but things happened in their lives that made it too difficult to keep up with the apprenticeship hours. These were working professionals with families. Things happened.

> "I had my afternoon hours that I could work on the stuff, but it all just boiled down to me not having time for my family when I was taking the courses. I think the bottom line was with my family structure. I shouldn't have taken more than one course at once....Then I had to put more time into the family, because I didn't put in as much as I should have, but I still had to put time in for them."

The particular challenge of the classes involving coding was the challenge of getting the programs exactly right. If you're a working professional who can allocate (say) three hours to a homework assignment, and a slip of the finger costs you one of those hours, you're in trouble.

> Andrew: "So if you get one little piece or spacing wrong, it doesn't work."

> John: "There were times that it would take me hours to find one comma out of place, or find that one something that was wrong, so I didn't mind sticking with it but it just got to the point where I just didn't get it."

Our current hypothesis is that we will have to change pedagogy if we're going to be able to use online classes to develop more high school computer science teachers. Apprenticeship leads to deep learning, but is not efficient. Apprenticeship makes sense if you are preparing software engineers, and the teacher can model expert software engineering practice. Software engineering practice is not the community of practice for high school computer science teachers. The practices and values of software engineers are not what motivates high school computer science teachers.

5.2.2   WHAT HIGH SCHOOL COMPUTER SCIENCE TEACHERS NEED TO SUCCEED

We should not duplicate the education we provide software engineers in order to develop high school computer science teachers. Using learner-centered design, we should instead explore what high school computer science teachers *want* to learn. Taking seriously the community of practice perspective of Lave and Wenger, we need to identify the practices and values at the center of the community of practice of high school computer science teachers.

To have high-quality and sustainable computing education in our schools, we need to develop *CS teacher identity* [225]. We want teachers to say, "I'm a computer science teacher." Teachers who express a teacher identity are more likely to be retained, more likely to join a professional organization, and more likely to seek out more professional learning opportunities [200]. The retention issue is particularly large. In the U.S., we lose about 50% of our science and mathematics teachers in the first five years. Our track record for retaining CS teachers is far worse [23].

Lijun Ni studied a group of teachers as they started attending CS teacher professional development. She followed them for a year, with interviews and surveys. Not all the teachers developed an identity as computer science teachers. In fact, some of them dropped out entirely. She used these case studies to develop a theory for what leads to an improved sense of identity [225, 226].

When Ni started with these teachers, they did not see themselves being CS teachers:

Rose[1]: "Really my degree is not in Computer Science. It's in Business Education. So, that's just my identity."

Mary: "Even though most of the courses I teach are Computer Science, I always say I'm a Business Education teacher. That's what I'm certified for."

They were hesitant to become CS teachers. They saw a lot of challenges. One was a lack of community. They already belonged to a community of practice (in business or mathematics). They don't recognize a community of practice of computer science teachers.

Cindy: "I don't have many colleagues in the county that I can turn to...I don't feel like there are...I've sat and I've talked to people...They all have their own way of wanting to do things (in CS)...We have a lot of people who are Business teachers with no idea what they're doing with this class."

John: "It would have been such an easy problem to solve if I would have been in a community of Computer Science teachers, because we would have talked about these things...I still think I'm a better Math teacher, just because I've had so much support. Whenever I have problems, I can talk with the people that I work with, most of who have taught for many years in Math. If we're eating lunch, every day, I'm eating with Math teachers. So, we can talk about our problems. With Computer Science, I've got nobody to talk to. I've learned so much about how to teach Math just in lunch conversations with other Math teachers."

Another was that they were underprepared. Teachers wanted to know more about computer science.

Becky: "I struggle with giving everyone the material and being able to explain it to everyone...I struggle with how to be creative with the programming. I have a problem with trying to make the programs have meaning to them... It is hard to teach. It's hard knowing how to teach it, how to give it to them. It's hard to explain. When I look at kid's codes, they think I should know it... They think that I should know it as soon

___

[1]All names are pseudonyms.

as I look at it. For the longest time I thought I should, but I don't have to. I have to study it just like they do. So, I would like some training."

Several teachers felt that computer science was too hard for most students. It was an elite subject.

May: "I think, computer science is more for really, really smart people. I'm not saying I'm smart, but I'm thinking that if I have to go take this Computer Science degree, that it's going to be really hard, because it's going to ask a lot of programming questions, syntax questions. I think computer science is a much higher level…When I say computing, I think of computing as being able to operate the computer…I believe that most students can successfully take and complete Computing in the Modern World, but it takes a little higher level of intelligence to complete the Introduction to Programming."

The teachers who did successfully develop a CS teacher identity in Ni's study joined a professional community in which there were *role models*, experienced and successful teachers who identified as CS teachers [225–227]. A group of CS teachers met one Saturday a month for several months to create course portfolios that described their practice, a form of *Disciplinary Commons* [310]. Ni found that having more expert teachers was particularly important for the new teachers who were developing a sense of identity as computing teachers. Teachers told Ni that "I want to be a CS teacher like Rita one day." The professional community gave teachers the opportunity to talk about their practice and share what they were learning.

Briana Morrison led a Disciplinary Commons for Computing Education (DCCE) where the community of teachers shared *recruitment practices* [219]. Since computer science is an elective subject in most states, teachers can only teach computer science if they are successful at recruiting students into their classes. Those teachers increased their enrollment over 300%! Having a community improved the practices that were important for these teachers.

Ni and Tom McKlin conducted an interview study of computer science teachers to identify the practices of successful and unsuccessful teachers [228]. Their bar for successful teachers was high.

- Successful teachers are *happy* in what they do and want to keep doing it.

- Successful teachers *recruit* students into their classes.

- Students of successful teachers *pass* the Advanced Placement CS exam. Ni and McKlin interviewed teachers who have *never* had a student pass the AP CS exam over several years of offering AP CS.

Here's a quote from an unsuccessful teacher on how she prepares students for the AP CS exam:

Everything in that class is more or less an assessment. They're supposed to read certain sections in the book, and then they have quizzes over the reading. After they do the reading assignments, they have case study quizzes and also case study segments of code that they will go in and manipulate to change to get the things in the case study to react different ways. Those are pretty much graded as labs or programs or quizzes.

What we see here is a focus on assessment and general strategies for teaching. The subject here could be mathematics or even history. The general strategy is not connected to computer science.

Here's the same question posed to a successful AP CS teacher.

And then if I read these (student quizzes), I can see any misconceptions or gaps in what I've done. I get a picture in my mind of where the current class is. Making them do the explaining is new this year. I'm seeing them do a lot better there. I'll do like little code (assignments) that they'll write once a week. They have to write it by hand away from the computer, and I'll read that and write them comments on what they're doing and help them grade it with a rubric, and also pass them back after I've read them for them to grade, too, and have them look at what was catching it or where it didn't quite get to it.

The successful teacher is attending to misconceptions. She does not talk about writing code. She reads code and comments on it. She has students reviewing each other's code. The strategy here is clearly about computer science.

5.2.3   DEVELOPING THE IDENTITY OF A COMPUTER SCIENCE TEACHER

Ni's work starts to paint a picture of the values and practices of the high school computer science teacher. It's different from what software engineers do and value. A teacher needs these pieces to develop an identity as a CS teacher.

- Teachers need a community of practice of CS teachers. It's important to develop their sense of identity. It's important to provide support for becoming a better computing teacher.

- Teachers need to be able to read and comment on code. Software Engineers need to do that, too, but they must also write code. We don't see successful CS teachers writing much code.

- Teachers care about learning to teach (pedagogical content knowledge). They want to know what students are typically going to get wrong, and how to address them. They want to know curricula.

- Developing teacher confidence in teaching computing is critical. We don't really know how much writing of program code is necessary to develop confidence as a teacher of program code. We know that computing teachers' confidence is related to their knowledge of programming and their pedagogical content knowledge.

5.2.4   DEVELOPING ONLINE TEACHER EDUCATION

We have continued our professional development efforts in the *CSLearning4U* project where our goal is to create new media for learning computer science at a distance by high school teachers. We are pursuing the correspondence school model of distance learning, rather than a remote classroom model [51]. A correspondence school model aims to provide materials that are designed to stand alone, while a remote classroom model places a camera in the place of a student's position in a classroom lecture—much as the camera filmed the play in early motion pictures (see Chapter 1). We aim to create a medium that can be studied, within the time constraints of high school teachers. An instructional medium for computer science to be used in a correspondence school model may also be useful to others, such as people re-entering the IT workforce [284]. What we are trying to show in our project is that we can design instruction, following principles of educational psychology, to help people learn computing better. Our results so-far are promising [205, 206, 218]. We are showing that it is not true that the only way to learn programming is by wrestling the interpreter or compiler.

We have built an electronic book (*ebook*) for learning computer science for high school teachers [91]. We mean it to feel like a book (sections, chapters, and parts, with little video) because teachers have experience with pacing their way through a book. They know how to fit that into their lives.

The ebook has features explicitly designed for teachers.

- It's a web-based ebook, available anywhere.

- Readers program within the ebook, without installing any additional software.

- We use an *examples+practice* structure for the ebook. The ebook interleaves worked examples and practice activities, based on research on the optimal pattern [318]. We believe that our ebook will lead to more efficient and effective learning than the more typical apprenticeship approach to learning programming, e.g., hours of struggle with syntax and errors [152].

- The ebook asks teachers to read code more than anything else, to answer questions about code, and to debug code. We use Parsons Problems [242] as a low cognitive load approach to practice programming (Figure 5.1). We give teachers programming problems, then give them all the correct lines of code for the solution on draggable tiles (in the left column) that have to be dragged into the right order and assembled (on the right). This problem requires understanding code, but never results in a syntax error. We rarely ask teachers to write a program from a blank screen. We are asking teachers to practice the skills that expert CS teachers practice, not the skills of software developers.

- The ebook includes support for "book clubs" or "reading groups." We want teachers to progress through the book with some fellow teachers (perhaps met through professional development or an organization meeting). The small groups interface lets the group collaboratively set reading goals, and shows progress toward those goals. The idea is to create social pressure to complete.

- The ebook includes teacher's notes which describe student learning challenges, how to diagnose them, and how to address them. We are aiming to provide pedagogical content knowledge. The book is clearly *for* teachers.

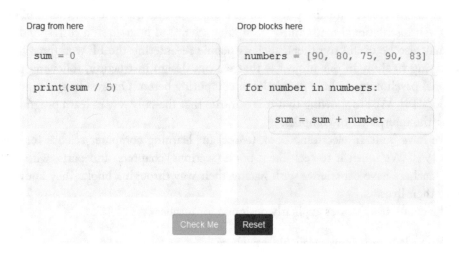

Figure 5.1: An example Parsons Problem.

Our results so far are promising, with good completion rates and evidence of learning [90]. What is most important is that the teachers are developing confidence. Teachers who engage in the ebook and use the facilities markedly improve their confidence in teaching computer science, even though our book is not centered around coding and apprenticeship [90].

An ebook is only one possible solution. I predict that the most successful solutions will take a learner-centered design approach. A successful solution will consider and respect the teacher's needs, what they know, and what they want to become.

5.3   DESIGNING COMPUTING EDUCATION FOR ADULTS

Adults are a challenging student audience. They have expertise and a community of practice. They have little time. Unlike students in school or higher education, adult learners know their community of practice, and they determine what they need to learn.

Relatively few adults want to become programmers. Many reject it. Teachers often do not want to become CS teachers, particularly if they are already successful in some other discipline. We have to ease the way.

A learner-centered design approach still works here.

- We begin with understanding what they are now, and what they want to become.

- We identify the challenges that they're facing, and start designing learning opportunities to address those.

- We have to respect the adult's time. This means that we will sometimes provide learning opportunities by embedding them in work situations. We have to provide efficient learning opportunities. (We should respect children's time, too, but the children have less opportunity to complain.)

- The goal sometimes isn't learning. Learning may be something that happens along the way. Teachers want to develop confidence in teaching computing. Graphic designers want to become more productive in their creative activities, while still enjoying what they do. We have to respect their goals in order to help them learn.

CHAPTER 6

Learner-Centered Computing Education for Computer Science Majors

The previous chapters explored what it meant to use a learner-centered design process to create computing education for people who are not necessarily aiming to be computing or IT professionals. End-users outside of the technology industry have a different community of practice that they participate in or want to join. Non-CS majors probably start from a different background than CS majors, and may harbor concerns about whether they belong in CS.

We can also use learner-centered design as a starting point when creating computing education opportunities for CS majors. We can design explicitly for learners who want to focus on computing. We start by characterizing the learners and their goals. We need to consider CS majors' needs, their learning challenges, what they know, and what they want to become.

- CS students don't really know about expert practice, but they want to be experts (i.e., central to a community of practice).

- CS students may have different learning goals. Not all will want to be programmers or software developers. Some may want to become different kinds of experts in the technology industry.

- CS majors don't all enter CS classes with the same background, and may harbor concerns about whether they belong in CS—just like non-CS majors.

6.1 MULTIPLE INTRODUCTORY COURSES ARE USEFUL

It's a good idea to have more than one introductory computing course at the higher-education level. At Georgia Tech, we decided to have three different introductory computing courses (see Chapter 4). This was an idea originally proposed in Margolis & Fisher's excellent book, *Unlocking the Clubhouse* [204], the story of increasing the proportion of women in the undergraduate computer science program at Carnegie Mellon University. They recommend having "alternative paths" into computing, based on interest and background.

Harvey Mudd College (HMC) has also developed multiple introductory courses, where they split between courses based on students' prior experience. HMC has had enormous success in increasing their proportion of women in CS to over 40%. They attribute part of their success to having these alternative paths [5].

It makes a difference because students have wildly different backgrounds in computing. Less than 10% of high schools in the U.S. have Advanced Placement Computer Science, and even where they have AP CS, it's overwhelmingly male and either white or Asian [87]. As Margolis & Fisher point out, men are more likely to "obsess" over computing and find the technology itself fascinating, while women tend to see computing as a tool and study it less obsessively. Jane Margolis refers to the greater background in computing that white or Asian males are more likely to have as "*preparatory privilege*" [203]. Women and under-represented minorities are less likely to have as much a computing background, and so are behind the white/Asian males even before the class started.

Preparatory privilege itself doesn't demand multiple introductory computing classes. Some students have greater mathematics background before entering Calculus 1, and some students may have read all of Charlotte Bronte's books before entering their first college Literature course. But in computer science, we have a unique culture which has been described as a *defensive climate* [15]. For example, students in computer science classes typically don't ask questions for clarification—they ask questions to show-off what they know. In an introductory course on Java, we might hear, "Sure, that's how constructors work in Java, but isn't Java a weaker language because it lacks the destructor in other C-based languages?" The question-asker in this example is not trying to improve their understanding of Java, but is trying to demonstrate their knowledge of other languages.

For students who have less background, the defensive climate can trigger a fear that they don't belong. If the students are already in a visible minority group, they may already have been fearing that they don't belong. It's not clear why the defensive climate developed. The defensive climate described by Barker at one school [15] has also been described in CS classes at other schools [193, 204]. If it is common across CS classes, it's better to keep separate those who have lots of knowledge to show-off from those lacking preparatory privilege.

In terms of drawing students into computing, HMC has an advantage that we don't have at Georgia Tech. Students at Harvey Mudd College don't declare a major until their second year. At Georgia Tech, students declare their major on their application form. That choice creates a disincentive for students to switch into computer science, even if they have a great experience in their first computing course. Students have already made a choice. Students at Georgia Tech do change majors, but they tend to change majors to a close major in which their existing coursework applies—a kind of loss aversion [166]. We get relatively few students switching into computer science after the Media Computation course.

6.2   THE "GEEK GENE"

A significant challenge to making CS majors classes open to a diverse range of students is that many computing educators believe that some students are "born" to program [192]. They believe that expertise in programming is genetic—that only some people have the *Geek Gene* [194]. Most CS teachers to whom I've asked the question are convinced some people can't learn to code. If ability to code is innate, then the job of the CS teacher can be defined as separating those who have the ability and those who don't, and teaching to those who do.

A belief that success in computing is due to innate differences is a significant hindrance to broadening participation in computing. Differences that a CS teacher sees, especially in undergraduate classes, are likely due to preparatory privilege. A 2015 study published in *Science* found that academic computer scientists believe that innate abilities are key to success in computing, more than do academics in statistics, biochemistry, physics, and most other disciplines [190]. Those disciplines with more belief in innate abilities had fewer female Ph.D.'s.

Raymond Lister has pointed out that it's very difficult to disprove or support the Geek Gene with empirical data [3]. We cannot track students from birth. Certainly, some students excel in computing from the start—but that alone isn't proof of a genetic difference. The Commonsense Computing group turned this question around to ask, "What do students know about computing *before* we teach them about programming?" Their series of research papers shows that students are remarkably successful at thinking through a variety of computational tasks, including sorting, searching, and even parallel processing [44, 191, 286]. The implication is that student difficulty with these concepts may arise more from how we teach and the difficulty of the programming languages for students.

Sources of difference in ability between students might be due to preparatory privilege and early access to *computers*. The difference could also be due to non-computing experiences. Great athletes have many experiences before formal training that develop their "innate" ability, like the basketball-obsessed child who dribbles a ball everywhere. Couldn't it be that there are analogous activities like dribbling-around-the-neighborhood that lead toward CS expertise? Consider the common pre-programming activity of writing the instructions out for making a peanut-butter-and-jelly sandwich, which is very often recommended in introductory courses [268, 303, 333]. If we believe that writing instructions for a sandwich helps to develop CS expertise, then other "writing instructions out" activities might lead toward CS expertise. Maybe people who seem to have genetic/innate ability in CS just did a lot of those kinds of activities before they got to our classes.

6.2.1   TEACHING TO ADDRESS DIFFERENCES

From a learner-centered design perspective, the cause of student differences is not the critical matter. A good teacher can reduce enormous differences in student abilities. *Teachers Matter* is the two-word title of a 2012 OECD report [232]. There is a difference between great teachers and poor teachers, and the difference can be seen in terms of student performance. All practice hours are not created equal. Hours spent in practice with a good teacher are going to contribute more to expertise than equivalent hours spent mucking around without a teacher. A good teacher can create opportunities for *deliberate practice* (i.e., practice which is focused on skills that need to be developed, as opposed to simple repetition of learned skills), which is the most critical factor leading to expertise [92].

We don't know the limits of good teaching. There is research evidence that we can use teaching to reduce differences that have been chalked up to genetics. Consider the fact that men have better spatial skills than women. Is it innate, or is it learned? It's not clear [223]. But the important point is: it doesn't matter. Terlecki, Newcombe, and Little have found that they can teach women to perform as well as men on visual skills and that the improvements in spatial ability both *transfers* and *persists* [311, 328]. Spatial skills are malleable and can be developed. Steve Cooper and his colleagues have shown that training computer science students in spatial skills had a significant impact on learning, and erased some differences due to race and wealth [47]. When spatial skills can be developed, they can have a positive impact on learning. Even if there are genetic differences between students in computing, we can likely teach skills that reduce or even eliminate differences.

It's obviously frustrating for computer science teachers to have seemingly no impact on some students. The award-winning Porter, Zingaro, and Lister ICER 2014 paper [255] points out that the earliest assessments in the class they studied correlate very highly with the final grade. If CS teachers follow common practice and it's unsuccessful for them, it's not surprising that they might believe, "I tried. I explained carefully. I gave interesting assignments. I gave good feedback. *It's got to be an innate trait. Some students are just born wired to program.*" The blog *Gas Station without Pumps* voiced a similar sentiment in a post [167]:

> But the outcomes for individual students seem to depend more on the students coming in than on what I do. Those students who come in better prepared or "innately" smarter progress faster than those who come in behind, so the end result of the teaching is that differences among the students are amplified, not reduced. Whether the differences in the students coming in are due to prior practice, prior teaching, or genetics is not really knowable, but also not really relevant.

The most important point in the above quote is that it's "not really relevant." If we can teach spatial ability, a skill that has a much stronger claim to being innate than programming, then we can likely teach people to program better. A good teacher using good methods can help students overcome some genetic/innate disparities. Claiming that their students don't have the right genes makes it too easy for teachers to give up. Rather, the goal in computing education should be to teach in order to develop expertise.

6.2.2   DIVERSE AND EFFECTIVE TEACHING METHODS

In general, computing teachers use too few teaching methods. Computing teachers are hesitant. I watch my own children taking CS classes, along with English, Chemistry, Physics, and Biology classes. In the CS classes, they write programs and get feedback. In the other classes, I see my children doing on-line interactive exercises, writing papers, using simulations, and working out problems in worksheets. If we only have one technique for teaching, we shouldn't be surprised if it doesn't always work. Several studies have supported the hypothesis that CS teachers are particularly unlikely to adopt new teaching approaches [14, 228].

My hypothesis is that we get poor results in computing classes because we use ineffective teaching methods. There is significant evidence that computing classes do have poor results. Introductory programming classes have higher-than-expected failure rates [20], in part because of the high degree of interactions in our curriculum and the way we teach it [266]. In both high school and undergraduate computer science classes, teachers can teach to the majority and be oblivious to the impact of teaching methods on the women and under-represented minorities in their classes [203, 204].

If we want to teach CS more effectively, we need to learn and develop better methods. If we don't strive for better methods, we're not going to get better results. Most computer science classes are based in lecture and programming assignments [15]. Fortunately, there are many methods in the research literature that have strong evidence for their benefits. Most of these fall under the description of *active learning*. A 2014 *Proceedings of the National Academy of Science* meta-analysis of over 200 papers stated unequivocally that active learning methods are far more effective for STEM student learning [105].

- *Peer instruction*: Peer instruction is where students respond to multiple choice questions (typically) in class and discuss the questions with peer students. The evidence in support of peer instruction is significant, across multiple classes [252, 287]. Peer instruction has had dramatic impacts on retention and reducing failure rates by half [251, 254].

- *Pair programming*: Pair programming is where two students work together at a single keyboard when working on programming exercises. Pair programming has been shown to have dramatic impacts on student learning and retention, even a full year after a pair programming class [209, 210, 253].

- *Worked examples*: Worked examples simply means providing students with more completely worked solutions, as opposed to more practice problems to solve [306]. Michael Caspersen developed the STREAM curriculum, drawing on several examples of best practice in computing education [41], and he used worked examples significantly [40]. Work at Georgia Tech has shown that the use of subgoal labels in worked examples significantly improves learning and retention, in both blocks-based and text programming languages [205, 218].

- *Games*: A growing body of work is showing the effectiveness of well-designed educational games to support student learning in computing. The first of these to show significant learning benefits was *Wu's Castle* which taught iteration [6, 79]. The results from Michael Lee's work on *Gidget* is compelling [186] [185–187, 189]. There is strong evidence that asking students to play an education video game is more likely to lead to learning than fighting with a programming assignment [188].

6.3   CREATING FACE-SAVING PATHS INTO COMPUTER SCIENCE

Computer science has a reputation. There is an expectation of what a computer scientist is like. In *Thinking, Fast and Slow*, Kahneman presents a description that he tells us he *designed* to seem like a computer scientist [165].

> Tom W is of high intelligence, although lacking in true creativity. He has a need for order and clarity, and for neat and tidy systems in which every detail finds its appropriate place. His writing is rather dull and mechanical, occasionally enlivened by somewhat corny puns and flashes of imagination of the sci-fi type. He has a strong drive for competence. He seems to have little feel and little sympathy for other people, and does not enjoy interacting with others. Self-centered, he nonetheless has a deep moral sense. (p. 147)

What happens if students want to learn computer science, but don't want to be labeled as "lacking in true creativity" and "dull and mechanical?" That is a challenge that many students face, especially those who do not fit the stereotype of being male and either white or Asian. These students may find the field of computing interesting, but not the expectations surrounding it. As mentioned earlier in the book, my colleagues Amy Bruckman and Betsy DiSalvo make the point like this [62]: "Computer science is not that difficult but wanting to learn it is."

Betsy DiSalvo created an intervention that was successful in engaging African American teen males in computer science [63, 153, 285]. She wanted to build on their interest in video games [61], and get them to see the game as a designed, constructed artifact. She hired African American teen males as *game testers* and undergraduate African American computer science students as "near-peer" mentors (close to the same age).

In the *Glitch Game Testers* project, participants were paid to come to the Georgia Tech campus, learn to be game testers, and then test games for local game studios. The Glitch teens were eager to play the latest-and-greatest video games. As game testers, their job was to find bugs in the games and to document those bugs so that the programmers could duplicate (and fix) the bugs. The Glitch teens wanted to learn more about computer science in order to do their jobs better—and also because they liked it. They didn't want to admit that to their family and friends, to whom studying computer science was not acceptable [64].

Glitch was a highly successful intervention. All 33 of the teens who enrolled in the project increased their CS knowledge and grew more interested in computing. All of them graduated high school, and more than half went on to study computer science in some form of post-secondary education.

A particularly interesting observation from Glitch is that the participants didn't tell their family and friends what they were doing. They were unwilling to tell anyone that they were learning about computer science. In her study, DiSalvo documented the *face-saving stories* that these students used to engage in an activity that they wanted to do. They told their friends that they were "being paid to play video games." They told their family that they had a paying job. They told their closest friends that they wanted to go to Georgia Tech to meet girls. Because they earned "points" for finding bugs, they told friends that they went in on Saturdays to earn more points toward valuable prizes—not to do more work, not to learn more about computer science.

DiSalvo found that Glitch offered face-saving paths into computer science [64]. Her participants did not want the labels and stigma that would follow a declaration of interest in academic computing. They found ways to make rational explanations about their activities to those whose opinions they valued. In Eccles' terms, they found a way to pursue achievement in computer science without engendering conflict with their identities, their stereotypes of the field, and their sense of success in the field.

Barbara Ericson built on DiSalvo's results in creating her *Project Rise Up 4 CS* [86]. African American pass rates on the Advanced Placement Computer Science exam lag behind whites or Hispanic students. Ericson wanted these students to get extra help, using a mentoring model like DiSalvo. Ericson designed her initiative on a program in Texas that had dramatically improved AP exam-taking [151]. She offered a monetary reward for attending a certain number of evening webinars, attending a certain number of face-to-face weekend workshops, and passing the AP CS exam.

In every region in which she's rolled out Project Rise Up, the African American pass rates have risen. It's hard to claim causation, though. She only reaches a dozen or two students in a state. Those students tell her about tutoring their friends with what they're learning, so the effect may be multiplicative. What's striking, though, is that students who earn the $100 (by completing the training and passing the exam) do not always take the money. When students are interviewed about Project Rise Up, they rarely mention the financial reward. Ericson is now running cohorts of Project Rise Up with different rewards (like video game consoles) or no rewards at all.

Financial incentives, face-saving techniques and near-peer mentors are ways in to computing for students who may not see it as part of their identity. Learner-centered design asks us to consider learners' needs, their sense of identity, and what they know and value. These techniques are ways of letting students study computer science without being called "dull" and "lacking creativity."

6.4 MORE THAN ONE KIND OF COMPUTER SCIENCE

A common theme in discussions about computer science education is to teach students "real" computer science. What's *real* computer science? I regularly interact with computing teachers who say that real programmers must "work with a text editor and a command line" [129], and that's what computing students should learn. A 1983 article in *Datamation* titled "Real Programmers Don't Use Pascal" [256] announced that real programmers use UNIX and FORTRAN. Users who care about computers being "personable" are "not real programmers." Even today, teachers tell their students that popular programming languages like PHP "aren't real programming languages" [301].

The problem is that there is more than one *real* computer science. There are many kinds of computer science today. The 1983 *Datamation* article says that real programmers work at NASA, NSA, or Boeing—but only a small percentage of programmers work there. As Scaffidi, Shaw, and Myers showed us [274], the vast majority of programmers aren't professional software developers at all. Bonnie Nardi in *A Small Matter of Programming* tells us about the wide range of different kinds of programmers that exist in any one enterprise, doing a wide variety of tasks [220]. Some of the most sophisticated programmers in Nardi's study developed macros for others to use in building Microsoft Excel spreadsheets—a task which is not possible in FORTRAN, using a text editor, at a command line.

6.4.1 THREADS

At Georgia Tech, we used this insight to change the way that we structured our undergraduate Bachelor of Science in Computer Science (B.S. in CS) degree [106]. Our degree at Georgia Tech was structured like most other B.S. in CS degrees—there was a core set of courses that everyone was required to take, and a set of specializations. We saw that there was "real computer science," and sub-fields within that.

We decided instead to think about computing as eight *Threads* of computer science, such as Intelligence, Information Internetworking, People, Theory, and Media [106]. The B.S. in CS at Georgia Tech is defined as completing the requirements for any *two* threads. We encourage students to think about the kind of job they wanted, and the kind of computer science they need to succeed at that job. If they want to study how multimedia can be compressed and transmitted efficiently, they might study Media and Theory. If they want to build tools for creative people to effectively design music and movies, they might study Media and People. If they want to think about developing intelligent agents that meet the needs of users, they might want to study Intelligence and People.

We did not define a *core* for the B.S. in CS. Instead, the faculty associated with each Thread were asked, "Tell me what courses students need to take to develop expertise in this Thread, within X credit hours." Some Thread faculty defined new courses, like *Prototyping Intelligent Appliances* where students build physical computing devices where the computers embedded within use AI algorithms and heuristics. But when we developed all the 24 possible combinations of two choices from eight Threads, we found that the first two years were the same for all paths. The core emerged rather than being designed in.

Students like Threads because they like to make choices. They like to think about what they might do with computing. They like to be able to choose which "real CS" they want to study. However, Mike Hewner's research suggests that they probably did not choose threads because of a desired occupation. They probably chose threads based on enjoyment of introductory courses.

6.4.2   HOW COMPUTER SCIENCE STUDENTS MAKE CHOICES

Mike Hewner studied how computer science students make their curricular choices [138, 141]. He started out studying what computer science majors know about computer science, and was surprised at the answers he got. We might expect beginning students not to understand CS, since there is little CS in high schools in the U.S. However, he found that even 3rd and 4th year students had significant misconceptions. He interviewed multiple third-year B.S. in CS students who told him that Computer Graphics was the study of Adobe Photoshop, which was why they didn't plan to ever take Graphics.

Given that CS students don't really understand CS, we might expect that they make ill-informed curricular choices. Hewner found that they were ill-informed, but they weren't necessarily bad. Hewner interviewed over a dozen CS students at three different universities. He analyzed the transcripts and other resources (like the descriptions of the curriculum provided to students) using an intensive technique called *grounded theory analysis* [321]. The goal of grounded theory analysis is to use a variety of materials (e.g., over a dozen interview transcripts, analyses of web pages describing the curriculum, etc.) to generate a theory, which might be tested in later experiments. Hewner developed a theory of how students make curricular choices [139].

The key insight is that *students use enjoyment as a proxy for affinity*. Students take classes that interest them, and if they enjoy the classes, they decide that they must be good at that topic. So they decide to pursue that major or specialization or Thread. The Georgia Tech Threads program offers an orientation course in which every Thread was introduced. Whether students enjoyed that treatment determined the students' choice of Threads.

Enjoyment was influenced by the quality of the specific teacher or teaching assistant, or maybe even the time of day that the class was offered (e.g., 8 am lectures might decrease the odds of enjoying that topic). Students told Hewner that they knew that their choices were being influenced by somewhat arbitrary factors such as which teacher they got and whether they liked the teacher, but they still believed that enjoyment implied affinity. Once they've made the choice, *they simply follow the curriculum*.

Hewner found that the CS students he interviewed didn't really know what CS was, or even know what kind of job they wanted. They did not know much about the community of practice that they wanted to join. Hewner found even third- and fourth-year students who didn't know the topics for the courses they were taking the next term. They simply trusted the curriculum.

In Betsy DiSalvo's work in Glitch, her game-testers were interested in learning about programming. They wanted to know what the programmers did when they received the Glitch students' bug reports. Betsy gave them some lessons on Alice and on Python, then asked them which they preferred [60]. There was not a clear winner. All of the Glitch students developed interests in computer science. Those who reported more interested in the design and graphical aspects preferred Alice. Those who reported more interested in what software engineers did preferred Python. Even within a small study like Glitch, there was more than one kind of computer science.

Considering DiSalvo's results in the light of Hewner's results, it's interesting to consider how the students developed these different interests. Hewner suggests that students come in to learning experiences like Glitch based on casual interest (as does Alexander's model for the development of expertise [4]), then have an experience where there is some contrast in terms of their enjoyment that allows them to develop more specific goals. Perhaps the causality worked in the opposite direction. Perhaps because students enjoyed Python, they developed software engineering interests, and other students who enjoyed Alice reported greater affinity for design or graphics interests. Hewner's research suggests that enjoyment in an introductory experience (which includes a first programming language) is critical for student choice to pursue that field.

6.5   CONTEXT HELPS COMPUTER SCIENCE MAJORS, TOO

In an earlier chapter, I wrote that contextualized computing education was important for improving student retention in our non-CS majors class at Georgia Tech, and at other schools, too. Contextualized computing education isn't just for the non-CS majors. It's helpful for the CS majors, too.

Allison Elliott Tew, Brian Dorn, and Bill Leahy ran a study to explore the role of context in teaching a course on computer organization [313]. The course is common in computer science curricula. The goal is for students to understand computing at the lowest levels, e.g., how memory works, how the central processing unit works, and how connections to input and output devices work. In our traditional course, we used a book that worked from bits up to programming languages, using an imaginary central processing unit (CPU) in the descriptions. Real central processing units are fairly complicated, so the imaginary one simplified some unnecessary complexity—it's a form of scaffolding.

In our new Bachelors of Computational Media, we wanted students to learn about low-level computing, but with the perspective of that degree. The parallel course taught how to program a Nintendo *Gameboy*. The Nintendo Gameboy is an under-powered computer, so you have to program it with an understanding of memory, CPU, how graphics are controlled on the Gameboy, and how the controller is read. It's a computer organization course, but contextualized around a real device. Students write programs that really run on a Gameboy.

Not all the topics are exactly the same between the two courses, but there is a sizable overlap. Tew, Dorn, and Leahy created a test that measured understanding on that overlap, and they surveyed the students for their attitudes about the course.

- There were no statistically significant differences in performance between the two classes.

- The Gameboy class *liked* the class more. Over 94% of the Gameboy class agreed that the class was "More fun than most" or "One of the most fun." 51% of the conventional class had similar agreement with those two statements.

- The Gameboy class reported doing more than was required with the assignments, because they were intriguing and fun. More time on task typically leads to more learning.

It's worthwhile contrasting this result with the Media Computation Data Structures class from back in Chapter 4. The results are similar, in that both groups of students found the content interesting by placing it in a context. Yarosh found that some students did not like the context in the Data Structures class. They wanted more content and felt that the context was a waste of time.

Tew, Dorn, and Leahy were comparing two different courses. Students who did not want the contextualized approach could take the more traditional course. Their results may have been more positive because there was a choice for students. In both cases, we have evidence that adding context to more advanced (not just introductory) courses can improve student engagement. The effect may not be the same for all students. Some students may not like the context.

A learner-centered design approach suggests that we start by studying our learners. We need to understand what motivates our learners, and provide education that addresses those motivations. Context is one of the tools we can use, and it can be effective even in more advanced classes.

6.6 THE NEED FOR GREATER EXPLORATION IN COMPUTING EDUCATION

As mentioned in Chapter 1, we at Georgia Tech created a new major in 2005, two years after the creation of the Media Computation course. The Bachelors in Computational Media (B.S. in CM) is the only joint undergraduate degree at Georgia Tech, between the College of Computing and the School of Literature, Media, and Communication in the Ivan Allen College of the Liberal Arts. It's a degree about the intersection of computing technology with the liberal arts.

The B.S. in CM degree is not directly related to the Media Computation course. In fact, B.S. in CM students don't take Media Computation courses. I do think it played a role in creating the opportunity for the CM degree. When over half of the liberal arts majors are dropping out or failing CS each semester, there is little interest in creating a joint degree. When we define a new kind of CS that engages liberal arts majors, we can start to ask the question, "What if we go further with this?"

The B.S. in CM and the B.S. in CS have essentially the same core computing courses. (One difference is the computer organization course, mentioned earlier in this chapter.) The B.S. in CM is over 40% female, while the B.S. in CS is less than 20% female. Why the difference? I suspect that part of the answer is that CM is about using computing as a tool to achieve a goal of human expression, and computing-as-tool is more a powerful perspective with many female students [204].

More importantly, the B.S. in CM is an important exploration of alternative models of computing education in higher-education. CM majors get good jobs with some of the highest starting salaries among majors at Georgia Tech. They have a different demographic. They get somewhat *different* jobs than CS majors. CM majors are about a different kind of CS.

We need to explore more options in how to learn and teach computer science. Too much of computing education is focused on teaching "real computer science" and how only some students are "born" to be programmers. We can teach more with better methods. We can reach more students by starting from a learner-centered design approach.

One of the ways that we should be exploring different ways to teach is by using other programming languages and tools. In 2014, Kathi Fisler presented a study showing that she had beaten the Rainfall Problem, described back in Chapter 2. Her introductory students (one group still in high school) did significantly better than other previously published studies [99], e.g., 74% of one group of students solved the problem without error, and 66% of another. She achieved this goal by teaching differently. She used a different programming language (e.g., Racket, a variant of Scheme) than past studies. She taught the students to program differently, using higher-level programming constructs than in previous studies. That worked. How many of our students' programming problems are artifacts of our programming language choices?

As mentioned earlier, Michael Lee has built and evaluated a video game that teaches programming [186]. One of his findings is that he could improve student retention by making the programming language "personable." He created an avatar for the computer which looked sad when it encountered an error, and happy when the program worked correctly. Students kept at the game and learned more when using the version of the game with the personable avatar. Remember the *Datamation* article that complained about users who wanted "personable" computers? Turns out that "personable" computers are *learnable* computers.

CHAPTER 7

Steps Toward Computing for Everyone

In this last chapter, I revisit the reasons from Chapter 1 on why to teach computing to everyone. I consider each of the levels of formal education: elementary school (roughly ages 1–13 in the U.S.), secondary/high school (ages 14–18), and undergraduate. The goals from Chapter 1 have different implications for each of those levels. I consider the issues in achieving those goals in terms of change at the different levels of education.

In this chapter, I focus on *formal* computing education. Informal computing education (e.g., online programs, after school programs, summer camps, museums, MOOCs, coding boot camps) is unlikely to reach *everyone*. Studies of informal computing education [34, 95, 143] have found many of them to be even more biased in favor of more wealthy and male students than current face-to-face computer science courses. We will reach a greater range of students and most likely achieve universal computing literacy through formal computing education pathways [130]. Informal computing education can play an important role in influencing identity and impacting perception of computing (consider expectancy-value theory here)[145], but are voluntary. They are more likely to be adopted by wealthier families [53], so we are more likely to have society-wide effects (and particularly, to broaden participation in computing) through the formal pathways— elementary school, secondary school, and higher education.

7.1 REVISITING WHY EVERYONE SHOULD LEARN COMPUTING

Here is the original list, with comments on each based on the research reviewed in the last six chapters.

- **Jobs**: We still need more software developers. The research evidence suggests that computing education increases the probability that a student will consider a career in computing.

- **Learn about their world**: The world is still increasingly dependent on computing technology. Computing education can inform students about the world they live in.

- **Computational thinking**: The original definition of computational thinking had two goals. One was about learning transferable knowledge from computing that could be applied in daily life. I presented evidence in Chapter 3 suggesting that that was unlikely. The second was about applying computing ideas to facilitate computing work in other disciplines, which is likely to be achieved and important.

- **Computational literacy**: By learning computing, we gain access to a powerful new form of expression that we can use to think about other domains. Mitchel Resnick argued that learning to code is like "learning to write" [262]. Scardamalia and Bereiter explained that the process of writing transforms the writer's knowledge [275]. Essentially, the goal of knowing about computing as a medium for learning in other disciplines is the same as the "application" part of computational thinking. I am going to use computational literacy going forward, since computational thinking has two meanings, only one of which is supported by research.

- **Productivity**: Computing education can make users more productive, and can reduce productivity costs caused by a lack of understanding of computing. These are outcomes of computational literacy. I collapse productivity as a reason for learning computing into computational literacy.

- **Broadening Participation**: Research evidence suggests that a lack of access to computing education prevents women and under-represented minorities from pursuing computing as a career. We need to provide equitable access to this economically important opportunity.

Based on the last six chapters, the six original reasons for providing computing education to everyone comes down to four: jobs, learning about their world, computational literacy, and broadening participation. I use those four in the following sections. (Note that the four reasons lead to different kinds of learning and teaching methods.)

- If you care about jobs, then the authenticity of the classroom activities matters. You want to prepare students for professional practice. But tools that are appropriate for professional practice may inhibit using computing as a medium for powerful, generative ideas. A tool that's great for software engineering may not also be great for learning physics.

- If you care about learning about the computing in their world, then having students seeing real computing matters. It makes sense to use computers like the BBC micro:bit, a barebones, pocket-sized computer with visible circuit board and chips which allow students to see the computer as it really is [16]. However, for computational literacy, it's the use of the computer that matters, not the device itself. For the goal of broadening participation, seeing circuits and chips may not attract women and members of under-represented groups who may be dissuaded from pursuing computing because of a "geek" perception.

- If you care about computational literacy, then you are unlikely to be concerned about authenticity from the perspective of a software industry community of practice. Learning about computing itself may not be as important as learning science, mathematics, or other subjects.

- If you care about broadening participation, then exposure to computing is important [111], but you want to describe the computing industry as it might be, not as it is now. Knowing how it is now is decidedly gender-biased [211] which might convince students that they don't want that kind of job.

7.2   TEACHING COMPUTING IN ELEMENTARY SCHOOL

Teaching computing in elementary/primary school guarantees that *everyone* gets access to computing education. Elementary school is where we guarantee our citizens literacy in text and in basic mathematics. Perhaps that is a reasonable place to also guarantee computing literacy.

Getting computer science into elementary schools is difficult in the U.S. because there is little agreement on what constitutes computer science. In some states, using a computer with office applications, Adobe Photoshop, or doing computer-aided design is considered computer science—which is unlikely to impact any of the reasons for teaching computing.

Considering our four reasons.

- *Jobs*: There is little that we can teach in elementary school that will directly be usable as a job skill years later. Technology changes rapidly, so we can't be sure what will be useful to teach a five year old that will be useful a dozen years or more later.

- *Learn about their world*: School children live in a computational world, and they are likely aware of it. We certainly should be able to teach them about the computing in their world. We don't know how much of it they will understand or retain.

- *Computational literacy*: This is perhaps the strongest reason for teaching computing at the elementary school level. As described in Chapter 3, we already have research evidence that we can teach elementary school children computing that can be useful to them in learning mathematics and science.

- *Broadening participation*: Research evidence suggests that introducing computing in school ages can engage women and under-represented minorities in computing. We don't know if it's more or less powerful in elementary school than in secondary school.

7.2.1   WHY NOT TEACH COMPUTING IN ELEMENTARY SCHOOL

Elementary school is certainly the best place to start for the goal of computational literacy (and probably for learning about their world and broadening participation). By starting early, the generative advantages of learning with coding can be used for a lifetime of education. It's why we start teaching reading and writing from the earliest ages—not as a job skill, but because it's a literacy that offers advantages throughout life. Early computing education is clearly the right goal.

However, we are so far away from that goal in the U.S. that we have to think in terms of a process to achieve that goal. Elementary school is probably the most *expensive* place to teach computing. Most elementary school grades are taught by a single teacher. Teaching all of those elementary-grade teachers enough about computing for them to have confidence in teaching it would be a much larger undertaking than the CS10K goal described in Chapter 5—which in itself does not reach the majority of U.S. high schools.

A different solution is to have a specialized computing teacher visit classes. Rather than prepare all teachers to teach computer science, we would only have to prepare one teacher per school. However, there are many more elementary schools than high schools or universities, so reaching everyone is still much more expensive at the elementary school level.

Later in the chapter, I suggest that we ought to start at the undergraduate level. If we teach everyone computing at university or college, we will reach all future teachers. Elementary school computing curriculum becomes much easier and less expensive to implement when teachers know something about computing. This process takes a generation, but is more sustainable than using in-service education to create many teachers.

An open research question is what an elementary school child can learn about computing and what should be taught at what ages. Jean Piaget's theory of cognitive development is notable for recognizing that children think *differently* than adults [249]. One of the hallmarks of those differences is that young children (typically, around 11 years old) do not engage in abstract reasoning. Computer science is primarily about building and reasoning about abstractions. We know relatively little about young children, before 11 years old, learning about programming. What in-the-field empirical evidence we have of young children programming shows very little use of abstract control structures, e.g., few loops or conditionals [32, 95, 161, 162]. Perhaps this implies that the kind of computing we teach in elementary school should have few of those kinds of traditional data structures.

7.2.2   WHY TEACH COMPUTING IN ELEMENTARY SCHOOL

One goal for computing education in elementary school is what Dan Schwartz calls *Preparation for Future Learning* [278]. Schwartz found that he could prepare students for learning in statistics by engaging them in games and activities that drew their attention to issues like distribution and sampling. Shuchi Grover used that perspective with middle school students (roughly 11–13 years old) to *prepare* them for learning computer science [117]. She did teach programming, but her goal was to influence transfer and more generalizable computational thinking [116], like the work of Sharon Carver discussed in Chapter 3.

Alan Kay's work has continued from the Logo, Smalltalk, and Boxer days described in Chapter 3. He has a novel solution to the problems of teaching computing education in elementary school. Rather than teach a traditional programming language, he proposes teaching a smaller set of powerful ideas that are generative in the sense that they can be used in combination to learn many topics in mathematics and science.

The Squeakland website[1] with the *Etoys* environment offers a set of example projects that describe the curricular progression that Kay has in mind [168]. He starts out with turtle graphics, for all the same reasons that Seymour Papert did. In Squeakland, anything the student draws can be a "turtle." Sample projects include controlling a student-drawn car, and extending the car with sensors. Notice that the code includes no iterative control structures. Instead of loops, the Squeakland examples make heavy use of multiple, parallel processes. The cars move because the small programs defining how they move and interact with their environment execute repeatedly by the system. The student-drawn car is controlled by a student-drawn steering wheel. Rotating the wheel changes the wheel's `heading` which is then the input for how much the car should turn. The sensors example can be the basis for building biological simulations of how animals sense their environment as described in Abelson and diSessa's *Turtle Geometry* book [2]. See Figure 7.1 for examples of each of these.

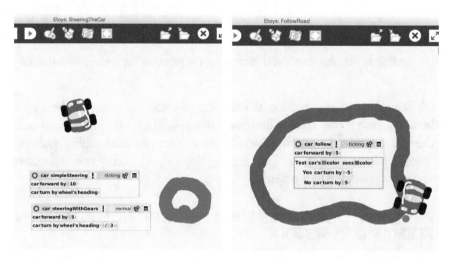

Figure 7.1: Using turtle graphics to control student-drawn objects and to use feedback to control the object.

As the projects develop, later projects shrink the turtle down to a particle. No new programming ideas are introduced. Instead, the same turtle graphics are used to control particles in simulations of how a drop of dye is diffused in water and of ideal gas laws (see Figure 7.2). StarLogo and NetLogo also allow students to explore having thousands of turtles, but do not also support manipulation of individual student-drawn turtles as cleanly [261, 323]. Having both provides easy access to students even at young grades, yet works for sophisticated concepts without introducing new computing ideas. It's a small core set of powerful ideas that can be used to learn a wide variety of concepts in science and mathematics.

[1]http://www.squeakland.org

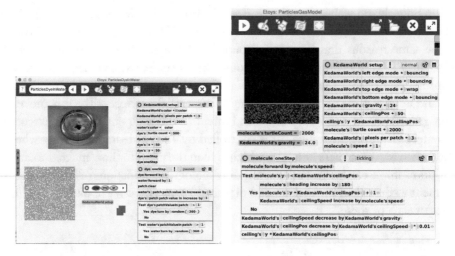

Figure 7.2: Scaling the turtles down and increasing the number for more sophisticated simulations.

Kay's Squeakland vision reduces the amount of computing that teachers need to learn to be confident. Teachers do not have to become conversant in a traditional programming language. Instead, they develop confidence using a smaller set of concepts. The learning goal of this approach is clearly computational literacy, not jobs. Scaling this vision to many teachers and many schools is an open research question and project.

7.2.3 RESEARCH QUESTIONS FOR TEACHING COMPUTING IN ELEMENTARY SCHOOL

Some of the research questions we need to answer about young children learning computing include the following.

- What are young children capable of learning from computing?

- Piaget suggested that his stages of development are based on the child's experience. Might experiencing computing (with the abstraction that is so common in programming) at early years advance cognitive development so that children could do abstract reasoning earlier? Would that abstract reasoning transfer outside of computing?

- Would knowledge of computing transfer from elementary school to later years? How does that answer change if the student does not have access to computing education in later years? That is, if there is no computing education in secondary school, what will the elementary school student still remember about computing when reaching undergraduate years?

- What powerful, generative ideas from computing might we teach at the elementary school level that could be useful in science and mathematics (and other) classes?

- What impact does computing education at the elementary level have on career choice later?

- How do the different learning goals interact at the elementary school level? If a teacher promoted computing for jobs, would it have a positive impact on broadening participation in computing? If a teacher promoted computational literacy, would students develop a positive outlook on computing careers?

- How do we best design programming languages and environments for elementary school students? Besides the Squeakland system, there are programming languages for children like Scratch [201] and Snap! [11], but we are still at an early stage of these explorations.

7.3   TEACHING COMPUTING IN SECONDARY SCHOOL

High/secondary school is another point at which we might teach everyone about computing. It's less expensive than trying to reach all elementary schools. Considering our four reasons for teaching computing to everyone in high school:

- *Jobs*: The jobs argument is stronger at the high school level. Studies of who uses programming suggest that it's not just in the technology industry. Many people will need some programming for their job. If we just consider jobs in the technology industry, it may be possible to prepare a high school student to take a job in the technology industry directly out of high school. We certainly know that high schools can well-prepare students for an undergraduate computing degree and success in the technology industry after graduation.

- *Learn about their world*: High school students are immersed in a computational world and likely to have the abstract reasoning abilities to make sense of it.

- *Computational literacy*: High school is the best chance to reach everyone to improve productivity and allows us to reduce computing illiteracy in order to enhance economic productivity. Computing can be a powerful tool for learning high school mathematics and science.

- *Broadening participation*: Research evidence suggests that introducing computing in high school can engage and motivate women and members of under-represented groups to pursue computing as a career and in undergraduate studies.

However, it's still very expensive to introduce computing in U.S. high schools. The UK Computing at School effort has a huge advantage. They already had an Information and Communications Technology (ICT) curriculum that computer science replaced. There were teachers in place, and a teacher preparation system in place. In the U.S., less than 10% of high schools have access to Advanced Placement Computer Science classes.

I was a principal investigator on Project *"Georgia Computes!"* (2006–2012) whose goal was to improve computing education across the entire state of Georgia [33, 132, 133]. We made a significant push to provide access to computing education at the high school level. In 2010, we attempted to measure the impact of the first four years of the project. We surveyed students in every introductory computing course across the University System of Georgia. 19 of the 29 public universities in Georgia that teach computing agreed to distribute our survey [134].

Our results supported the value of high school computing education. High school computer science classes made a difference for women and under-represented minorities. Those students were much more likely to have had high school computer science experience than the male students. The *Institute for Computing Education* (ICE) offered professional development as part of "Georgia Computes!" (GaComputes) 36% of all high schools in Georgia had at least one teacher who attended ICE professional development. The GaComputes high schools (the 36% who had a teacher who took our professional development) produced 57% of the undergraduate students taking computing courses in our survey. The GaComputes high schools produced the majority of the female and under-represented minority students who took our survey.

These results also point out just how expensive it will be. "Georgia Computes!" cost about $6 million USD. It's likely that the 36% of schools we reached were the *easiest* schools to reach. The other two-thirds of schools would cost significantly more, e.g., the remaining schools are in more rural areas, and they will likely require different kinds of approaches. (The inverse Lake Wobegon effect applies here, too—the schools we reached tended to be richer than the ones we did not.) It will be very expensive to place a computing teacher in every high school so that every child gets access to computing. The CS10K effort was introduced in Chapter 5. There are somewhere between 25,000 and 30,000 high schools in the U.S., so the CS10K effort is only going to reach a portion of the high schools in the United States. A single teacher alone is unlikely to be retained (see below), so a more sustainable model is to have multiple teachers per school—thus increasing the cost.

It's difficult to convince a high school teacher to become a computer science teacher, as described in a previous chapter. Lijun Ni interviewed teachers considering becoming computer science teachers, and came up with a list of concerns [225].

- Because there are so few computer science teachers, they lack a community. They don't have fellow teachers to discuss the challenges in their classroom.

- Computer science class *content* changes often. A mathematics or physics teacher can count on the content remaining mostly the same over many years, so that the teacher can focus on teaching *better*. A computer science teacher also has to deal with changing programming languages and tools.

- A good computer science teacher often develops the computing knowledge sufficient to work in the computing industry—for significantly more income.

For all these reasons, retention of high school computing teachers is likely to be a significant problem. In general, in the U.S., only about 50% of high school teachers in science, mathematics, and engineering/technology subjects are retained past five years [150]. We know less about computer science teachers. The Exploring CS (ECS) group reported on a cohort of 81 computer science teachers who attended professional development five years previously. Only 40 of those teachers were still teaching ECS [23]. Recent estimates in the U.S. suggest that computer science teachers will be retained in the classroom for only about three years [331].

If we were going to put computer science teachers into every high school in the U.S., we need to have computer science in college and university education programs. Preparing high school teachers is the job of schools and departments of education in colleges and universities. We cannot hope to sustain computing education at high schools across all of the U.S. entirely through providing professional development to existing teachers.

We prepare new teachers and sustain existing teachers through our post-secondary education programs. I do not know of a study of computer science education in teacher preparation programs in the U.S. From my informal discussions, there are less than a dozen education faculty who work in computing education, and only a small percentage of those have teacher development programs. We are not yet ready to sustain universal computing literacy through high schools in the U.S.

7.3.1 RESEARCH QUESTIONS FOR TEACHING COMPUTING IN SECONDARY SCHOOL

Some of the research questions we need to answer about high school students learning computing include the following.

- What can we teach to *everyone*? The inverse Lake Wobegon effect biases us to think that we know about everyone based on the students that we already see, but we see a small, privileged segment of the overall population. For example, do cognitive impairments limit the amount of computing that can be learned? What part of computing can be taught to everyone?

- How do we reach all the high school teachers that we need to prepare in the U.S.? How do we incentivize them to become computing teachers? What are the costs of reach everywhere, including rural areas?

- What are the questions that high school students have about computing in their world? Can we answer these without programming?

- How do we design programming languages and environments to serve our goal of computational literacy, without assuming the goal of jobs? Will students find these programming languages and environments authentic if they are not in professional practice?

7.4   TEACHING COMPUTING TO UNDERGRADUATES

We could teach computing to all undergraduates across the U.S. much more cheaply and with much better understanding of what we're doing than at elementary or high school levels. We already have computer science teachers at most colleges and universities in the U.S. and through much of the world. To teach all undergraduates would require growth in existing departments, not creating new departments at new schools. We know more about teaching computer science to undergraduates, than to elementary or high school students. We can better anticipate the problems and plan to address them.

The argument for teaching all undergraduates about computing is stronger than for teaching all elementary or high school students. Alan Perlis first made the argument in 1961 that computing was valuable for every undergraduate (as described in Chapter 3). Perlis argued that computer science is the study of process which impacts all disciplines at a university, and that programming was the best way to understand computer science. All four of the reasons for teaching computing to everyone (jobs, learning about their world, computational literacy, and broadening participation) can be addressed with undergraduates.

If we revisit Scaffidi, Shaw, and Myers (Chapter 1) [274] and think about the vast number of users who will program without being software developers, those users are likely to earn a bachelors degree. The kinds of activities that Scaffidi and colleagues describe (e.g., doing database queries, building models in spreadsheets, using modeling and simulation in science or engineering) typically require post-secondary education. If we want to aim computing education at the people whom we can be most certain are going to need it, then undergraduate education is the place to develop computing literacy.

A required course in computing education for all undergraduates would improve computing literacy across levels. For example, all teachers at one point were undergraduates. By teaching all undergraduates, you also reach all teachers. If all teachers already had a first course, having all high schools and elementary schools include computing education becomes more economically viable. We know that attitudes about computing change dramatically with only a single course [111, 133]. By creating a required course for all undergraduates, all students get the opportunity to see computing and decide if it's something that they're interested in. We would create possibilities.

We will only reach everyone with a *required* course, not an elective. Female students are much less likely to take an elective computer science course than a required one [9]. Requirements matter because we are Humans, not Econs [165]. We don't make rational decisions. Opportunities that we should explore but don't know anything about (like computer science) are unlikely to be explored voluntarily.

A single course in computer science at the undergraduate level can only have so much impact. Consider Hewner's study described in Chapter 4 [140]. A single course is unlikely to convince someone with a *negative* impression of computing that programming is fun. A single course is unlikely to lead to integrating computing across liberal arts, sciences, business, and architecture. We'd have to change the faculty to change their teaching, too, which is a very difficult problem [133]. But it's a great first step.

Making computing education a requirement for *all* undergraduates in the U.S. demands changes in how and what we teach. At the undergraduate level, all four of our possible reasons for teaching computing are valid. A learner-centered design approach suggests that we respect the students' learning goals and prepare them for the community of practice that they want to join. The pedagogy of the classes would have to change. The tools and languages would have to change and improve.

7.4.1   IMPROVE TEACHING ABOUT COMPUTING

Most computing education today occurs in higher education. Computer science teaching at the higher-education level today is mostly focused on jobs, specifically, to prepare students to be software developers [14, 15]. To improve how students learn computing, we need to change and improve computer science teaching.

Computer science teachers at the undergraduate level who focus on teaching are relatively rare. Professors are people who generally love to learn. That's how they get that job. However, they don't all love to learn about teaching, particularly if that learning involves changing how they teach. Our results in trying to teach higher education computing teachers in Georgia is that only a small percentage are actively interested in improving their teaching [133].

Changing the perspective of computing teachers is hard because it is a change to their goals. Consider an analogy with championship athletics and public health. Computing teachers take pride in where their students get jobs. A recent article talks about a New York City CS teacher who hangs t-shirts along his walls from the companies where his students find jobs [36]. That image reminds me of the championship banners and trophies in the coach's office. Computing education today is mostly about creating stars, the computational elite who go on to the big leagues like Google, Facebook, Amazon, and Apple. Teaching everyone is more about public health. Instead of producing only the elite, our focus is on making sure that everyone's health is improved. It's less about producing stars than it is making sure that everyone avoids smoking and gets exercise. The former is more exciting. The latter has greater economic and social impact. The general public is more excited about the former. The public is interested in the next Steve Jobs. What we most need are more successful, computationally literate citizens.

Computer science faculty are rarely well-versed in how human learning actually occurs. We mostly teach how we were taught, or how we wish we were taught. Even those who have taught for years often rationalize their educational decisions with a "folk pedagogy" view of education [195]. They may have a sense for what works and what doesn't in our classes, but they might not know learning theory or have empirical evidence that supports their perspectives.

Computing teachers rarely use empirical evidence when deciding what to teach. Davide Fossati and I studied 14 CS higher-education teachers from three institutions [104]. Davide asked them about times they made a change in their teaching practice. Why did they make the change, and how did they know if it was successful or not? The most common story was that they wanted to make a change, or that they'd talked to a few students and they had suggested a change. Nobody surveyed all the students. Not a single teacher used evidence such as whole class performance on a test or homework.

Lecia Barker conducted a larger study (interviews with 66 CS faculty across 36 institutions) about how they adopted new teaching practices [14]. She found that, "Despite being researchers themselves, the CS faculty we spoke to for the most part did not believe that results from educational studies were credible reasons to try out teaching practices." Like the Fossati study, Barker found that teachers used practices based on individual student's feedback, not based on empirical data. In contrast, a 2010 study found that over 80% of physics teachers (700 surveyed) were familiar with one or more research-backed teaching practices [50].

The importance of changing teaching methods is even greater when the goal is to teach a diverse range of students. The *New York Times* ran an article that followed up on the PNAS 2014 meta-study about active learning [105], "Are College Lectures Unfair?" [243]. The point is that active learning is particularly important when trying to create more equitable opportunities for students.

> Research comparing the two methods has consistently found that students over all perform better in active-learning courses than in traditional lecture courses. However, women, minorities, and low-income and first-generation students benefit more, on average, than white males from more affluent, educated families.

To change the teaching experience for most students, teachers have to design for someone other than ourselves. We have to be learner-centered, e.g., we should design our teaching based on empirical evidence about our students and about how learning works [59]. We need to gather data from the learners, because it's far too easy to talk to a couple of people who are like us and assume that they represent the norm [12].

If we want to teach computing to all undergraduates, computer science teachers would have to take teaching non-majors seriously. They would have to trust data more than their expertise, which is biased by their expert blind spot [221]. They would have to learn to be open to learning new methods. They would need to use a learner-centered design approach.

7.4.2   IMPROVE THE TOOLS OF COMPUTING

The programming tools used in today's computer classes are there because they are similar to ones used in the software industry. New languages that are becoming more common in undergraduate computing classes are only getting there because of their use in industry. But when our students are not planning to enter the software industry, we have to re-think our motivations.

An impressive set of programming tools has been developed from a learner-centered perspective [172]. Scratch [201, 202] and Squeak Etoys [168] were both explicitly created to meet the needs of children-as-programmers, with different learning goals than becoming professional software developers. All the design decisions for Quorum were made using empirical usability data, especially with students, to make it provably usable for learners [302]. Smalltalk was explicitly designed to be a programming language "for children of all ages" [169, 170].

diSessa's Boxer [65] was designed to answer the question, "What should a programming tool look like if the goal is computational literacy, not professional software development?" diSessa wasn't interested in people building apps in Boxer. He wanted students to explore mathematics, physics, and their everyday computing needs. Boxer has a radically different design than most programming tools. It's designed to be understandable. It does not integrate with source code control systems or revision systems. It does not support type checking or unit testing. It's meant to be a tool for exploration and expression. Boxer is a programming tool to think with.

In this book, I have mentioned several exemplars for what a computing for everyone might look like. Boxer is one model. We might also look at the work of Michael Lee and Andrew Ko on *Gidget*, as mentioned at the end of the last chapter. Gidget is a video game that requires programming to progress through levels. Lee worked hard on the design of Gidget and came up with lessons that inform how we think about non-game programming tools, too. For example, Lee found that *personifying* the programming tool improves retention [186]. When Gidget sees a syntax error, the programmer is not informed "Missing semicolon" or "Malformed expression." Instead, Gidget says "I don't know what this is, so I'll just go on to the next step" and the avatar for Gidget looks *sad* that she was unable to do what the programmer asked her to do. The personification of the programming tool dramatically improved the number of game levels completed. They kept going. Personification makes the programming tool more welcoming.

While Boxer does not support type checking or explicit testing, that may be a mistake. Programmers make errors. End-user programmers likely make *more* errors. Because end-user programmers are not professional software developers, they are *less* likely to notice errors. Because they are often occasional programmers, they have less experience and ability in fixing errors. In comparison with the professional software developer, an error in a model or a simulation might be more expensive for the scientist, engineer, or business analyst who might want to use programming as part of their job.

Shriram Krishnamurthi and his team are drawing on research from end-user programming studies to develop a programming language that is accessible to all, but in which casual errors are less common [178]. It's meant to look like popular programming languages for students (like Python), but it has support for testing and powerful type systems to help the programming tool to help the user catch errors. We don't yet have the empirical evidence to tell us what's most important for non-CS programmers. These are important directions to explore.

If we are going to convince faculty in *non-CS* departments that their students, their majors, should take a course in computer science, we have to make changes. We have to change the way we teach. We have to change our tools. We have to think about different kinds of abstractions, and about the ways that non-CS-focused users interleave different kinds of artifacts into their computing process [54]. A learner-centered design approach can provide a starting point in making these changes.

7.4.3   CREATE MORE RESEARCHERS IN COMPUTING EDUCATION

The ACM SIGCSE International Computing Education Research (ICER) conference has never had more than 120 attendees. The conference moves between the U.S., Europe, and Australasia. There are more computing education researchers in Europe and Australasia, but attendance is higher when the conference is in the U.S. All told, though, that's a small number of people to study something which is increasingly being mandated in schools.

We need more people studying computing education. We need people to build good tools and teach better, as I previously stated. We also need researchers to determine if the tools and teaching methods are effective. We need researchers developing theory to inform the creation of new tools and better methods.

Sally Fincher has led an enormous capacity-building effort in computing education world-wide. She has led several efforts in the United States and Australasia to develop more computing education researchers [98]. She then led the effort to create the ICER conference so that those researchers would have a venue and a community. She is the editor of the journal *Computer Science Education*. She literally wrote the book *Computer Science Education Research* [97].

The effort to grow more computing education researchers needs more Sally's, but needs institutionalization of these efforts. There are a handful of universities around the world where one can earn a Ph.D. doing computing education research. Having so few researchers means that we see too few contexts, and we study too few kinds of students. Having such a small number of researchers makes us too susceptible to the inverse Lake Wobegon effect. It's hard to know what we don't know.

7.5   CONCLUSION: LEARNER-CENTERED DESIGN OF COMPUTING EDUCATION

I argue in these chapters that universal computational literacy is important and desirable. To achieve that goal, we have to change the way that we design computing education. We need a learner-centered design process, rather than assuming that we have homogeneous learners who all share the goal of becoming expert programmers and professional software developers.

A learner-centered design process for computing education includes (at least) the following.

- Understanding of *where the learners are starting from and what they want to do*—what they know, what they want to achieve (e.g., the community of practice they hope to join), and how they see themselves (e.g., their identity).

- Understanding of *where the learners are likely to have trouble*—start designing to address what learners are going to have difficulty doing or understanding.

- Understanding of *the differences among the learners*. There will likely be variance in prior knowledge and experiences, motivations, and goals among your learners.

- *Use of language that the learners understand.* Do not presume that learners know expert terminology—or even want to learn it. Not all those who program want to be called "programmers."

- *Contextualization* to make abstract concepts more concrete and related to learners' interests and values.

- *Scaffolding* to reduce complexity and guide process.

- *Expecting the learners to change.* Literacy is a new identity. When learners develop an identity as computationally literate users, or even end-user programmers, they are different. Designing for different learners is a new process.

The implication is that no one programming environment or curriculum will meet all learner needs. My colleague, Jim Foley, suggested that Computing will likely split into subdisciplines like Engineering, because there is as much intellectual diversity in Computing and its uses as in the different kinds of Engineering. Once upon a time, undergraduates would get degrees in "Engineering." Today, they get degrees in "Mechanical Engineering" or "Civil Engineering" or any of another dozen forms. Jim argues that we will have that one day in Computing. We can expect that those different forms of Computing will prefer different notations, tools, and curricula.

Computational literacy is too powerful as a tool for thinking and creative expression to be held by a small number of people. Powerful tools eventually become part of our common culture. Maybe it will take decades, or even hundreds of years. There was a long time between the development of the printing press and the ability of common people to read and write. Computing education research is just starting, and there is a lot to explore.

Bibliography

[1] AAUW. *Tech-Savvy: Educating Girls in the New Computer Age.* American Association of University Women Education Foundation, 2000. 55

[2] H. Abelson and A. DiSessa. *Turtle geometry: The computer as a medium for exploring mathematics.* MIT press, 1986. 41, 99

[3] A. Ahadi and R. Lister. Geek genes, prior knowledge, stumbling points and learning edge momentum: parts of the one elephant? In *ICER '13: Proceedings of the ninth annual international ACM conference on International computing education research*, pages 123–128, New York, NY, USA, 2013. ACM. DOI: 10.1145/2493394.2493416. 85

[4] P. A. Alexander. The development of expertise: The journey from acclimation to proficiency. *Review of Educational Research*, 32(8):10–14, 2003. 33, 92

[5] C. Alvarado and Z. Dodds. Women in CS: an evaluation of three promising practices. In *Proceedings of the 41st ACM technical symposium on Computer science education*, SIGCSE '10, pages 57–61, New York, NY, USA, 2010. ACM. DOI: 10.1145/1734263.1734281. 84

[6] J. R. Anderson, F. Conrad, A. T. Corbett, J. M. Fincham, D. Hoffman, and Q. Wu. *Computer programming and transfer*, pages 205–234. Lawrence Erlbaum Associates, Hillsdale, NJ, 1993. 29, 87

[7] O. Astrachan, J. Cuny, C. Stephenson, and C. Wilson. The CS10K project: Mobilizing the community to transform high school computing. In *Proceedings of the 42nd ACM Technical Symposium on Computer Science Education*, SIGCSE '11, pages 85–86, New York, NY, USA, 2011. ACM. DOI: 10.1145/1953163.1953193. 74

[8] W. F. Atchison, S. D. Conte, J. W. Hamblen, T. E. Hull, T. A. Keenan, W. B. Kehl, E. J. McCluskey, S. O. Navarro, W. C. Rheinboldt, E. J. Schweppe, W. Viavant, and D. M. Young, Jr. Curriculum 68: Recommendations for academic programs in computer science: A report of the ACM curriculum committee on computer science. *Communications of the ACM*, 11(3):151–197, Mar. 1968. DOI: 10.1145/362929.362976. 12

[9] C. R. Baker. Computer science classes in high school: why too few kids take them. http://national.deseretnews.com/article/909/computer-science-classes-in-high-school-why-too-few-kids-take-them.html, January 2014. 104

[10] T. Balch, J. Summet, D. Blank, D. Kumar, M. Guzdial, K. O'Hara, D. Walker, M. Sweat, G. Gupta, S. Tansley, J. Jackson, M. Gupta, M. N. Muhammad, S. Prashad, N. Eilbert, and A. Gavin. Designing personal robots for education: Hardware, software, and curriculum. *IEEE Pervasive Computing*, 7(2):5–9, Apr. 2008. DOI: 10.1109/MPRV.2008.29. 64

[11] M. Ball, L. Mock, J. McKinsey, Z. Machardy, D. Garcia, N. Titterton, and B. Harvey. Oh, Snap! enabling and encouraging success in CS1 (abstract only). In *Proceedings of the 46th ACM Technical Symposium on Computer Science Education*, SIGCSE '15, pages 691–691, New York, NY, USA, 2015. ACM. DOI: 10.1145/2676723.2691947. 101

[12] L. Barker and J. Gruning. The student prompt: Student feedback and change in teaching practices in postsecondary computer science. In *Proceedings of the 2014 Frontiers in Education Conference*, 2014. DOI: 10.1109/FIE.2014.7044464. 106

[13] L. Barker, C. Hovey, and L. Thompson. Results of a large-scale, multi-institutional study of undergraduate retention in computing. In *Frontiers in Education Conference (FIE), 2014 IEEE*, pages 1–8, Oct 2014. DOI: 10.1109/FIE.2014.7044267. 65

[14] L. Barker, C. L. Hovey, and J. Gruning. What influences CS faculty to adopt teaching practices? In *Proceedings of the 46th ACM Technical Symposium on Computer Science Education*, SIGCSE '15, pages 604–609, New York, NY, USA, 2015. ACM. DOI: 10.1145/2676723.2677282. 23, 87, 105, 106

[15] L. J. Barker, K. Garvin-Doxas, and M. Jackson. Defensive climate in the computer science education. In D. Knox, editor, *The Proceedings of the Thirty-third SIGCSE Technical Symposium on Computer Science Education, 2002*, pages 43–47. ACM, 2002. 10, 84, 87, 105

[16] BBC. Introducing the BBC micro:bit. http://www.bbc.co.uk/programmes/articles/4hVG2Br1W1LKCmw8nSm9WnQ/introducing-the-bbc-micro-bit, 2015. 96

[17] T. Bell, P. Andreae, and A. Robins. Computer science in New Zealand high schools: the first year of the new standards. In *Proceedings of the 43rd ACM technical symposium on Computer Science Education*, SIGCSE '12, pages 343–348, New York, NY, USA, 2012. ACM. DOI: 10.1145/2157136.2157240. 1

[18] T. Bell, P. Andreae, and A. Robins. A case study of the introduction of computer science in nz schools. *Transactions on Computing Education*, 14(2):10:1–10:31, June 2014. DOI: 10.1145/2602485. 1, 74

[19] K. Benda, A. Bruckman, and M. Guzdial. When life and learning do not fit: Challenges of workload and communication in introductory computer science online. *ACM Transactions on Computing Education*, 12(4):1–38, 2012. DOI: 10.1145/2382564.2382567. 74

[20] J. Bennedsen and M. E. Caspersen. Failure rates in introductory programming. *SIGCSE Bulletin*, 39(2):32–36, 2007. DOI: 10.1145/1272848.1272879. 54, 87

[21] C. Bereiter and M. Scardamalia. *The psychology of written composition*. Routledge, 2013. 7, 41, 46, 48

[22] T. Berners-Lee. *Weaving the Web: The original design and ultimate destiny of the World Wide Web by its Inventor*. Harper, San Francisco, CA, 1999. 6

[23] D. Bernier and J. Margolis. The revolving door: Computer science for all and the challenge of teacher retention. http://www.exploringcs.org/wp-content/uploads/2014/04/The-Revolving-Door-CS-for-All-and-the-Challenge-of-Teacher-Retention-Final.pdf, July 2014. 76, 103

[24] D. Berrett. The day the purpose of college changed. http://chronicle.com/article/The-Day-the-Purpose-of-College/151359/, January 2015. 13

[25] M. Biggers, A. Brauer, and T. Yilmaz. Student perceptions of computer science: a retention study comparing graduating seniors with CS leavers. In *ACM SIGCSE Bulletin*, volume 40, pages 402–406. ACM, 2008. DOI: 10.1145/1352322.1352274. 65

[26] A. F. Blackwell, J. A. Rode, and E. F. Toye. How do we program the home? gender, attention investment, and the psychology of programming at home. *International Journal of Human-Computer Studies*, 67(4):324–341, Apr. 2009. DOI: 10.1016/j.ijhcs.2008.09.011. 8

[27] P. C. Blumenfeld, E. Soloway, R. W. Marx, J. S. Krajcik, M. Guzdial, and A. Palincsar. Motivating project-based learning: Sustaining the doing, supporting the learning. *Educational Psychologist*, 26(3 & 4):369–398, 1991. DOI: 10.1080/00461520.1991.9653139. 66

[28] R. Bornat, S. Dehnadi, and Simon. Mental models, consistency and programming aptitude. In *Proceedings of the Tenth Conference on Australasian Computing Education - Volume 78*, ACE '08, pages 53–61, Darlinghurst, Australia, Australia, 2008. Australian Computer Society, Inc. 32

[29] A. L. Brown. Design experiments: Theoretical and methodological challenges in creating complex interventions in classroom settings. *The Journal of the Learning Sciences*, 2(2):141–178, 1992. DOI: 10.1207/s15327809jls0202_2. 40, 47

[30] N. C. C. Brown, M. Kölling, T. Crick, S. Peyton Jones, S. Humphreys, and S. Sentance. Bringing computer science back into schools: lessons from the UK. In *Proceeding of the 44th ACM technical symposium on Computer science education*, SIGCSE '13, pages 269–274, New York, NY, USA, 2013. ACM. DOI: 10.1145/2445196.2445277. 1, 13

[31] N. C. C. Brown, S. Sentance, T. Crick, and S. Humphreys. Restart: The resurgence of computer science in UK schools. *ACM Transactions on Computing Education*, 14(2):9:1–9:22, June 2014. DOI: 10.1145/2602484. 74

[32] A. Bruckman. *MOOSE Crossing: Construction, community, and learning in a networked virtual world for kids*. Ph.D. thesis, MIT Media Lab, 1997. 98

[33] A. Bruckman, M. Biggers, B. Ericson, T. McKlin, J. Dimond, B. DiSalvo, M. Hewner, L. Ni, and S. Yardi. "Georgia computes!": improving the computing education pipeline. In *SIGCSE '09: Proceedings of the 40th ACM technical symposium on Computer science education*, pages 86–90, New York, NY, USA, 2009. ACM. DOI: 10.1145/1508865.1508899. 102

[34] L. Buechley. Eyeo 2014: Thinking about making - an examination of what we mean by making (makeing) these days. https://vimeo.com/110616469, November 2014. 95

[35] Bureau of Labor Statistics. Occupational outlook handbook: Software developers. http://www.bls.gov/ooh/computer-and-information-technology/software-developers.htm, 2012. 3

[36] D. Cahn and J. Cahn. The godfather of public computer science education. http://www.huffingtonpost.com/david-cahn/the-godfather-of-public-c_b_8038722.html, August 2015. 105

[37] M. J. Canup and R. L. Shackelford. Using software to solve problems in large computing courses. In *Proceedings of the Twenty-ninth SIGCSE Technical Symposium on Computer Science Education*, SIGCSE '98, pages 135–139, New York, NY, USA, 1998. ACM. DOI: 10.1145/273133.273178. 53

[38] S. M. Carver. *Transfer of LOGO Debugging Skill: Analysis, Instruction, and Assessment*. Ph.D. thesis, Carnegie Mellon University, Pittsburgh, PA, 1986. 47

[39] S. M. Carver and D. Klahr. Assessing children's LOGO debugging skills with a formal model. *Journal of Educational Computing Research*, 2(4):487–525, 1986. DOI: 10.2190/KRD4-YNHH-X283-3P5V. 47

[40] M. E. Caspersen, J. Börstler, A. Decker, and C. Alphonce. Worked examples for sound OO pedagogy: the seventh "killer examples" workshop. In *OOPSLA Companion '08: Companion to the 23rd ACM SIGPLAN conference on Object-oriented programming systems languages and applications*, pages 781–782, New York, NY, USA, 2008. ACM. DOI: 10.1145/1449814.1449888. 87

[41] M. E. Caspersen and M. Kolling. STREAM: a first programming process. *Transactions on Computing Education*, 9(1):1–29, 2009. DOI: 10.1145/1513593.1513597. 87

[42] M. E. Caspersen and P. Nowack. Computational thinking and practice: A generic approach to computing in Danish high schools. In A. Carbone and J. Whalley, editors, *The 15th Australasian Computer Education Conference (ACE 2013)*, Adelaide, South Australia, February 2013. Conferences in Research and Practice in Information Technology (CRPIT). 1, 74

[43] A. Cenavskis. In San Francisco, computer science for all...soon. http://hechingerreport.org/san-francisco-plans-to-be-first-large-district-to-bring-computer-science-to-all-grades/, 2015. 1

[44] T.-Y. Chen, G. Lewandowski, R. McCartney, K. Sanders, and B. Simon. Commonsense computing: Using student sorting abilities to improve instruction. In *Proceedings of the 38th SIGCSE Technical Symposium on Computer Science Education*, SIGCSE '07, pages 276–280, New York, NY, USA, 2007. ACM. DOI: 10.1145/1227504.1227408. 85

[45] Chicago Business. Computer science coming to all Chicago Public Schools. http://www.chicagobusiness.com/article/20141208/NEWS08/141209789/computer-science-coming-to-all-chicago-public-schools, 2014. 1

[46] Computing Research Association. 2012–2013 Taulbee survey. *Computing Research News*, 26(5), 2014. 8

[47] S. Cooper, K. Wang, M. Israni, and S. Sorby. Spatial skills training in introductory computing. In *Proceedings of the Eleventh Annual International Conference on International Computing Education Research*, ICER '15, pages 13–20, New York, NY, USA, 2015. ACM. DOI: 10.1145/2787622.2787728. 86

[48] Creative Urban + Culture. A new department marks the rise of a discipline: 'Computational media'. http://creativeuc.net/college/2014/11/29/a-new-department-marks-the-rise-of-a-discipline-computational-media, December 2014. 17

[49] Q. Cutts, S. Esper, and B. Simon. Computing as the 4th "R": A general education approach to computing education. In *Proceedings of the Seventh International Workshop on Computing Education Research*, ICER '11, pages 133–138, New York, NY, USA, 2011. ACM. DOI: 10.1145/2016911.2016938. 40

[50] M. Dancy and C. Henderson. Pedagogical practices and instructional change of physics faculty. *American Journal of Physics*, 78(10):1056–1063, October 2010. DOI: 10.1119/1.3446763. 106

[51] J. S. Daniel. *Mega-Universities and Knowledge Media: Technology Strategies for Higher Education*. Kogan Page, London, 1996. 79

[52] T. H. Davenport and L. Prusak. *Information ecology: Mastering the information and knowledge environment*. Oxford University Press, 1997. 73

[53] P. E. Davis-Kean. The influence of parent education and family income on child achievement: the indirect role of parental expectations and the home environment. *Journal of Family
Psychology*, 19(2):294, 2005. DOI: 10.1037/0893-3200.19.2.294. 95

[54] E. Deitrick, R. B. Shapiro, M. P. Ahrens, R. Fiebrink, P. D. Lehrman, and S. Farooq.
Using distributed cognition theory to analyze collaborative computer science learning.
In *Proceedings of the Eleventh Annual International Conference on International Computing
Education Research*, ICER '15, pages 51–60, New York, NY, USA, 2015. ACM. DOI:
10.1145/2787622.2787715. 107

[55] P. Denning, D. E. Comer, D. Gries, M. C. Mulder, A. B. Tucker, A. J. Turner, and P. R.
Young. Computing as a discipline: preliminary report of the ACM task force on the core of
computer science. *ACM SIGCSE Bulletin*, 20(1):41–41, 1988. DOI: 10.1145/52965.52975.
2

[56] P. Denning and C. Martell. *Great Principles of Computing*. MIT Press, 2015. 40

[57] P. J. Denning. The profession of it: Beyond computational thinking. *Communications of the
ACM*, 52(6):28–30, June 2009. DOI: 10.1145/1610252.1610265. 4

[58] P. J. Denning, D. E. Comer, D. Gries, M. C. Mulder, A. Tucker, A. J. Turner, and P. R.
Young. Computing as a discipline. *Communications of the ACM*, 32(1):9–23, Jan. 1989.
DOI: 10.1145/63238.63239. 2

[59] I. Diethelm, P. Hubieser, and R. Klaus. Students, teachers and phenomena: Educational
reconstruction for computer science education. In R. McCartney and M. Laakso, editors,
12th Koli Calling conference on computing education research, 2012. 106

[60] B. DiSalvo. Graphical qualities of educational technology: Using drag-and-drop and text-
based programs for introductory computer science. *Computer Graphics and Applications,
IEEE*, 34(6):12–15, Nov 2014. DOI: 10.1109/MCG.2014.112. 91

[61] B. DiSalvo and A. Bruckman.   Race and gender in play practices: young African
American males.   In *FDG '10: Proceedings of the Fifth International Conference on the
Foundations of Digital Games*, pages 56–63, New York, NY, USA, 2010. ACM. DOI:
10.1145/1822348.1822356. 88

[62] B. DiSalvo and A. Bruckman.   From interests to values.   *Communications of the ACM*,
54(8):27–29, 2011. DOI: 10.1145/1978542.1978552. 33, 88

[63] B. DiSalvo, M. Guzdial, C. Meadows, K. Perry, T. McKlin, and A. Bruckman. Workifying
games: successfully engaging African American gamers with computer science. In *SIGCSE
'13: Proceeding of the 44th ACM technical symposium on Computer science education*, pages 317–
322, New York, NY, USA, 2013. ACM. DOI: 10.1145/2445196.2445292. 88

[64] E. DiSalvo, A. Bruckman, M. Guzdial, and T. McKlin. Saving face while geeking out: Navigating motivations of non-learners. *Journal of the Learning Sciences*, 23(3):269–315, 2014. 88, 89

[65] A. diSessa. *Changing Minds*. MIT Press, 2001. 1, 42, 107

[66] A. A. diSessa. A principled design for an integrated computational environment. *Human-Computer Interaction*, 1(1):1–47, 1985. DOI: 10.1207/s15327051hci0101_1. 42

[67] A. A. diSessa and H. Abelson. Boxer: A reconstructible computational medium. *Communications of the ACM*, 29(9):859–868, 1986. DOI: 10.1145/6592.6595. 43

[68] A. A. diSessa, D. Hammer, B. L. Sherin, and T. Kolpakowski. Inventing graphing: Meta-representational expertise in children. *Journal of Mathematical Behavior*, 2(117–160), 10. 43

[69] Disney Bloggers. 10 things you didn't know about The Lion King. http://blogs.disney.com/oh-my-disney/2014/10/11/10-things-you-didnt-know-about-the-lion-king/, November 2014. 66

[70] M. S. Donovan, J. D. Bransford, and J. W. Pellegrino. *How People Learn: Bridging Research and Practice*. National Academy Press, Washington DC, 1999. 27, 28

[71] B. Dorn. ScriptABLE: supporting informal learning with cases. In *ICER '11: Proceedings of the seventh international workshop on Computing education research*, pages 69–76, New York, NY, USA, 2011. ACM. DOI: 10.1145/2016911.2016927. 72, 73

[72] B. Dorn and M. Guzdial. Graphic designers who program as informal computer science learners. In *ICER '06: Proceedings of the second international workshop on Computing education research*, pages 127–134, New York, NY, USA, 2006. ACM. DOI: 10.1145/1151588.1151608. 71

[73] B. Dorn and M. Guzdial. Discovering computing: perspectives of web designers. In *ICER '10: Proceedings of the Sixth international workshop on Computing education research*, pages 23–30, New York, NY, USA, 2010. ACM. DOI: 10.1145/1839594.1839600. 71

[74] B. Dorn and M. Guzdial. Learning on the job: characterizing the programming knowledge and learning strategies of web designers. In *CHI '10: Proceedings of the SIGCHI Conference on Human Factors in Computing Systems*, pages 703–712, New York, NY, USA, 2010. ACM. DOI: 10.1145/1753326.1753430. 72

[75] B. Dorn, A. E. Tew, and M. Guzdial. Introductory computing construct use in an end-user programming community. In *VLHCC '07: Proceedings of the IEEE Symposium on Visual Languages and Human-Centric Computing*, pages 27–32, Washington, DC, USA, 2007. IEEE Computer Society. DOI: 10.1109/VLHCC.2007.35. 71, 73

[76] B. J. Dorn. *A case-based approach for supporting the informal computing education of end-user programmers.* Ph.D. thesis, College of Computing, Georgia Institute of Technology, Atlanta, GA, 2012. 7, 72

[77] B. Du Boulay. Some difficulties of learning to program. *Journal of Educational Computing Research*, 2(1):57–73, 1986. DOI: 10.2190/3LFX-9RRF-67T8-UVK9. 50

[78] B. Du Boulay, T. O'Shea, and J. Monk. The black box inside the glass box: presenting computing concepts to novices. *International Journal of Man-Machine Studies*, 14(3):237–249, 1981. DOI: 10.1016/S0020-7373(81)80056-9. 2, 31, 50

[79] M. Eagle and T. Barnes. Wu's castle: teaching arrays and loops in a game. In *ACM SIGCSE Bulletin*, volume 40, pages 245–249. ACM, 2008. DOI: 10.1145/1384271.1384337. 87

[80] J. S. Eccles. Understanding women's educational and occupational choices: Applying the Eccles et al model of achievement-related choices. *Psychology of Women Quarterly*, 18(585–609), 1994. DOI: 10.1111/j.1471-6402.1994.tb01049.x. 35

[81] J. S. Eccles. Who am I and what am I going to do with my life? personal and collective identities as motivators of action. *Educational Psychologist*, 44(2):78–89, 2009. DOI: 10.1080/00461520902832368. 35

[82] J. S. Eccles and R. D. Harold. Gender differences in sport involvement: applying the Eccles' Expectancy–Value Model. *Journal of Apple Sport Psychology*, 3(7–35), 1991. DOI: 10.1080/10413209108406432. 34

[83] C. English. Parents, students want computer science education in school. http://www.gallup.com/poll/184637/parents-students-computer-science-education-school.aspx, August 2015. 1

[84] N. L. Ensmenger. *The computer boys take over: Computers, programmers, and the politics of technical expertise.* MIT Press, Cambridge, MA, 2010. 12, 13

[85] B. Ericson. Is computing just for men? http://www.aauw.org/2015/03/11/is-computing-just-for-men/, March 2015. 3

[86] B. Ericson, S. Engelman, T. McKlin, and J. Taylor. Project Rise Up 4 CS: Increasing the number of Black students who pass advanced placement CS A. In *Proceedings of the 45th ACM Technical Symposium on Computer Science Education*, SIGCSE '14, pages 439–444, New York, NY, USA, 2014. ACM. DOI: 10.1145/2538862.2538937. 89

[87] B. Ericson and M. Guzdial. Measuring demographics and performance in computer science education at a nationwide scale using AP CS data. In *Proceedings of the 45th ACM Technical Symposium on Computer Science Education*, SIGCSE '14, pages 217–222, New York, NY, USA, 2014. ACM. DOI: 10.1145/2538862.2538918. 74, 84

[88] B. Ericson, M. Guzdial, and M. Biggers. A model for improving secondary CS education. In *SIGCSE '05: Proceedings of the 36th SIGCSE technical symposium on Computer science education*, pages 332–336, New York, NY, USA, 2005. ACM Press. DOI: 10.1145/1047344.1047460. 74

[89] B. Ericson, M. Guzdial, and M. Biggers. Improving secondary CS education: progress and problems. *SIGCSE Bulletin*, 39:298–301, March 2007. DOI: 10.1145/1227504.1227416. 74

[90] B. Ericson, S. Moore, B. Morrison, and M. Guzdial. Usability and usage of interactive features in an online ebook for CS teachers. In *Proceedings of the Workshop in Primary and Secondary Computing Education*, WiPSCE '15, pages 111–120, New York, NY, USA, 2015. ACM. DOI: 10.1145/2818314.2818335. 80

[91] B. J. Ericson, M. J. Guzdial, and B. B. Morrison. Analysis of interactive features designed to enhance learning in an ebook. In *Proceedings of the Eleventh Annual International Conference on International Computing Education Research*, ICER '15, pages 169–178, New York, NY, USA, 2015. ACM. DOI: 10.1145/2787622.2787731. 74, 79

[92] K. A. Ericsson, R. T. Krampe, and C. Tesch-Römer. The role of deliberate practice in the acquisition of expert performance. *Psychological Review*, 100(3):363, 1993. DOI: 10.1037/0033-295X.100.3.363. 86

[93] M. Felleisen, R. B. Findler, M. Flatt, and S. Krishnamurthi. *How to design programs*. MIT Press Cambridge, 2001. 53, 56

[94] M. Felleisen and S. Krishnamurthi. Viewpoint: Why computer science doesn't matter. *Communications of the ACM*, 52(7):37–40, July 2009. DOI: 10.1145/1538788.1538803. 49

[95] D. A. Fields, M. Giang, and Y. Kafai. Programming in the wild: Trends in youth computational participation in the online Scratch community. In *Proceedings of the 9th Workshop in Primary and Secondary Computing Education*, WiPSCE '14, pages 2–11, New York, NY, USA, 2014. ACM. DOI: 10.1145/2670757.2670768. 95, 98

[96] S. Fincher, R. Lister, T. Clear, A. Robins, J. Tenenberg, and M. Petre. Multi-institutional, multi-national studies in CSEd research: some design considerations and trade-offs. In *ICER '05: Proceedings of the first international workshop on Computing education research*, pages 111–121, New York, NY, USA, 2005. ACM. DOI: 10.1145/1089786.1089797. 23

[97] S. Fincher and M. Petre. *Computer Science Education Research*. CRC Press, 2004. 14, 108

[98] S. Fincher and J. Tenenberg. Using theory to inform capacity-building: Bootstrapping communities of practice in computer science education research. *Journal of Engineering Education*, 95(4):265–277, 2006. DOI: 10.1002/j.2168-9830.2006.tb00902.x. 108

[99] K. Fisler. The recurring rainfall problem. In *Proceedings of the Tenth Annual Conference on International Computing Education Research*, ICER '14, pages 35–42, New York, NY, USA, 2014. ACM. DOI: 10.1145/2632320.2632346. 94

[100] A. E. Fleury. Programming in Java: Student-constructed rules. In *Proceedings of the Thirty-first SIGCSE Technical Symposium on Computer Science Education*, SIGCSE '00, pages 197–201, New York, NY, USA, 2000. ACM. DOI: 10.1145/330908.331854. 32

[101] A. Forte. Programming for communication: overcoming motivational barriers to computation for all. In *HCC '03: Proceedings of the 2003 IEEE Symposium on Human Centric Computing Languages and Environments*, pages 285–286, Washington, DC, USA, 2003. IEEE Computer Society. DOI: 10.1109/HCC.2003.1260252. 61

[102] A. Forte and M. Guzdial. Computers for communication, not calculation: Media as a motivation and context for learning. In *HICSS '04: Proceedings of the Proceedings of the 37th Annual Hawaii International Conference on System Sciences (HICSS'04) - Track 4*, page 40096.1, Washington, DC, USA, 2004. IEEE Computer Society. DOI: 10.1109/HICSS.2004.1265259. 6, 56, 60

[103] A. Forte and M. Guzdial. Motivation and nonmajors in computer science: identifying discrete audiences for introductory courses. *IEEE Transactions on Education*, 48(2):248–253, 2005. DOI: 10.1109/TE.2004.842924. 61, 65

[104] D. Fossati and M. Guzdial. The use of evidence in the change making process of computer science educators. In *Proceedings of the 42nd ACM Technical Symposium on Computer Science Education*, SIGCSE '11, pages 685–690, New York, NY, USA, 2011. ACM. DOI: 10.1145/1953163.1953352. 105

[105] S. Freeman, S. L. Eddy, M. McDonough, M. K. Smith, N. Okoroafor, H. Jordt, and M. P. Wenderoth. Active learning increases student performance in science, engineering, and mathematics. *Proceedings of the National Academy of Sciences*, 111(23):8410–8415, 2014. DOI: 10.1073/pnas.1319030111. 29, 87, 106

[106] M. Furst, C. Isbell, and M. Guzdial. Threads: how to restructure a computer science curriculum for a flat world. In *SIGCSE '07: Proceedings of the 38th SIGCSE technical symposium on Computer science education*, pages 420–424, New York, NY, USA, 2007. ACM. DOI: 10.1145/1227504.1227456. 90

[107] J. Gal-Ezer and C. Stephenson. The current state of computer science in U.S. high schools: A report from two national surveys. *Journal for Computing Teachers*, 2009. 13

[108] J. Gal-Ezer and C. Stephenson. A tale of two countries: Successes and challenges in K-12 computer science education in Israel and the United States. *Transactions on Computing Education*, 14(2):8:1–8:18, June 2014. DOI: 10.1145/2602483. 74

[109] D. Goldberg, D. Grunwald, C. Lewis, J. Feld, K. Donley, and O. Edbrooke. Addressing 21st century skills by embedding computer science in K-12 classes. In *Proceeding of the 44th ACM Technical Symposium on Computer Science Education*, SIGCSE '13, pages 637–638, New York, NY, USA, 2013. ACM. DOI: 10.1145/2445196.2445384. 6

[110] J. Goody and I. Watt. The consequences of literacy. In J. Goody, editor, *Literacy in Traditional Societies*, pages 304–345. Cambridge University Press, Cambridge, England, 1968. 6

[111] Google CS Ed Research group. Women who choose computer science–what really matters: The critical role of encouragement and exposure. Technical report, Google, 2014. 65, 97, 104

[112] J. Gray, K. Haynie, S. Packman, M. Boehm, C. Crawford, and D. Muralidhar. A mid-project report on a statewide professional development model for CS Principles. In *Proceedings of the 46th ACM Technical Symposium on Computer Science Education*, SIGCSE '15, pages 380–385, New York, NY, USA, 2015. ACM. DOI: 10.1145/2676723.2677306. 74

[113] T. R. G. Green. Conditional program statements and comprehensibility to professional programmers. *Journal of Occupational Psychology*, 50:93–109, 1977. DOI: 10.1111/j.2044-8325.1977.tb00363.x. 59

[114] I. Greenberg, D. Kumar, and D. Xu. Creative coding and visual portfolios for CS1. In *Proceedings of the 43rd ACM Technical Symposium on Computer Science Education*, SIGCSE '12, pages 247–252, New York, NY, USA, 2012. ACM. DOI: 10.1145/2157136.2157214. 64

[115] M. Greenberger. *Computers and the World of the Future*. MIT Press, 1962. 1, 37

[116] S. Grover. *Foundations for advancing computational thinking: Balanced designs for deeper learning in an online computer science course for middle school students*. Ph.D. thesis, Stanford University, 2014. 98

[117] S. Grover, R. D. Pea, and S. Cooper. Expansive framing and preparation for future learning in middle-school computer science. In *ICLS 2014 Proceedings*. International Society for the Learning Sciences, International Society for the Learning Sciences, 2014. 98

[118] M. Guzdial. Software-realized scaffolding to facilitate programming for science learning. *Interactive Learning Environments*, 4(1):1–44, 1995. DOI: 10.1080/1049482940040101. 44

[119] M. Guzdial. *Squeak: Object-oriented design with Multimedia Applications*. Prentice-Hall, 2001. 58

[120] M. Guzdial. Using Squeak for teaching user interface software. In *The Proceedings of the Thirty-second SIGCSE Technical Symposium on Computer Science Education*, pages 219–223. ACM Press, 2001. DOI: 10.1145/364447.364588. 58

[121] M. Guzdial. A media computation course for non-majors. In *ITiCSE '03: Proceedings of the 8th annual conference on Innovation and technology in computer science education*, pages 104–108, New York, NY, USA, 2003. ACM. DOI: 10.1145/961511.961542. 18

[122] M. Guzdial. *Introduction to Computing and Programming in Python: A Multimedia Approach*. Prentice-Hall, Upper Saddle River, NJ, 2004. 56

[123] M. Guzdial. Education: Teaching computing to everyone. *Communications of the ACM*, 52(5):31–33, May 2009. DOI: 10.1145/1506409.1506420. 53

[124] M. Guzdial. Does contextualized computing education help? *ACM Inroads*, 1(4):4–6, 2010. DOI: 10.1145/1869746.1869747. 64

[125] M. Guzdial. Defining: What does it mean to understand computing? https://computinged.wordpress.com/2012/05/24/defining-what-does-it-mean-to-understand-computing/, May 2012. 2

[126] M. Guzdial. Exploring hypotheses about media computation. In *ICER '13: Proceedings of the ninth annual international ACM conference on International computing education research*, pages 19–26, New York, NY, USA, 2013. ACM. DOI: 10.1145/2493394.2493397. 18, 60, 63, 65

[127] M. Guzdial. The most gender-balanced computing program in the USA: Computational media at Georgia Tech. https://computinged.wordpress.com/2014/09/02/the-most-gender-balanced-computing-program-in-the-usa/, September 2014. 17

[128] M. Guzdial. The bottleneck in increasing accessibility to CS education is producing enough CS teachers. http://cacm.acm.org/blogs/blog-cacm/192586-the-bottleneck-in-increasing-accessibility-to-cs-education-is-producing-enough-cs-teachers/fulltext, October 2015. 74

[129] M. Guzdial. Do blocks equal "making" and text equal "coding"? doing mediacomp in blocks-based languages. https://computinged.wordpress.com/2015/07/08/do-blocks-equal-making-and-text-equal-coding/, July 2015. 89

[130] M. Guzdial. Plain talk on computing education. *Communications of the ACM*, 58(8):10–11, July 2015. DOI: 10.1145/2788449. 95

[131] M. Guzdial and B. Ericson. *Introduction to Computing and Programming in Java: A Multimedia Approach*. Prentice-Hall, 2005. 59

[132] M. Guzdial and B. Ericson. Georgia Computes!: an alliance to broaden participation across the state of Georgia. *ACM Inroads*, 3(4):86–89, Dec. 2012. DOI: 10.1145/2381083.2381104. 74, 102

[133] M. Guzdial, B. Ericson, T. Mcklin, and S. Engelman. Georgia Computes!: An intervention in a US state, with formal and informal education in a policy context. *Transactions on Computing Education*, 14(2):1–29, 2014. DOI: 10.1145/2602488. 13, 102, 104, 105

[134] M. Guzdial, B. J. Ericson, T. McKlin, and S. Engelman. A statewide survey on computing education pathways and influences: factors in broadening participation in computing. In *ICER '12: Proceedings of the ninth annual international conference on International computing education research*, pages 143–150, New York, NY, USA, 2012. ACM. DOI: 10.1145/2361276.2361304. 3, 8, 102

[135] M. Guzdial and A. Forte. Design process for a non-majors computing course. In *SIGCSE '05: Proceedings of the 36th SIGCSE technical symposium on Computer science education*, pages 361–365, New York, NY, USA, 2005. ACM. DOI: 10.1145/1047344.1047468. 56, 61

[136] M. Guzdial and A. E. Tew. Imagineering inauthentic legitimate peripheral participation: an instructional design approach for motivating computing education. In *Proceedings of the second international workshop on Computing education research*, ICER '06, pages 51–58, New York, NY, USA, 2006. ACM. DOI: 10.1145/1151588.1151597. 14, 62

[137] I. Harel and S. Papert. Software design as a learning environment. *Interactive Learning Environments*, 1(1):1–32, 1990. DOI: 10.1080/1049482900010102. 43, 50

[138] M. Hewner. *Student conceptions about the field of computer science*. Ph.D. thesis, College of Computing, Georgia Institute of Technology, Atlanta, GA, October 2012. 91

[139] M. Hewner. Undergraduate conceptions of the field of computer science. In *Proceedings of the Ninth Annual International ACM Conference on International Computing Education Research*, ICER '13, pages 107–114, New York, NY, USA, 2013. ACM. DOI: 10.1145/2493394.2493414. 91

[140] M. Hewner and M. Guzdial. Attitudes about computing in postsecondary graduates. In *ICER '08: Proceeding of the fourth international workshop on Computing education research*, pages 71–78, New York, NY, USA, 2008. ACM. DOI: 10.1145/1404520.1404528. 65, 104

[141] M. Hewner and M. Guzdial. How CS majors select a specialization. In *Proceedings of the International Computing Education Research Workshop*, New York, NY, 2011. ACM, ACM. DOI: 10.1145/2016911.2016916. 91

[142] C. E. Hmelo and M. Guzdial. Of black and glass boxes: Scaffolding for learning and doing. In D. C. Edelson and E. A. Domeshek, editors, *Proceedings of the International Conference of the Learning Sciences 1996*, pages 128–134, Charlottesville, VA, 1996. Assocation for the Advancement of Computing in Education. 44

[143] A. D. Ho, I. Chuang, J. Reich, C. A. Coleman, J. Whitehill, C. G. Northcutt, J. J. Williams, J. D. Hansen, G. Lopez, and R. Petersen. HarvardX and MITx: Two years of open online courses Fall 2012–Summer 2014. *Available at SSRN 2586847*, 2015. 95

[144] D. Holland and K. Leander. Ethnographic studies of positioning and subjectivity: An introduction. *Ethos*, 32(2):127–139, 2004. DOI: 10.1525/eth.2004.32.2.127. 66

[145] M. S. Horn. The role of cultural forms in tangible interaction design. In *Proceedings of Tangible, Embedded, and Embodied Interaction (TEI'13)*, pages 117–124. ACM Press, ACM Press, 2013. DOI: 10.1145/2460625.2460643. 95

[146] S. Horwitz. And on to Java. http://apcentral.collegeboard.com/apc/members/courses/teachers_corner/17135.html, 2002. 23

[147] A. Hubbard and Y. Kao. Industry partnerships to support computer science high school teachers' pedagogical content knowledge. In *Proceedings of the 15th Annual Conference on Information Technology Education*, SIGITE '14, pages 89–90, New York, NY, USA, 2014. ACM. DOI: 10.1145/2656450.2656481. 74

[148] P. Hubwieser, J. Magenheim, A. Mühling, and A. Ruf. Towards a conceptualization of pedagogical content knowledge for computer science. In *Proceedings of the Ninth Annual International ACM Conference on International Computing Education Research*, ICER '13, pages 1–8, New York, NY, USA, 2013. ACM. DOI: 10.1145/2493394.2493395. 33

[149] C. D. Hundhausen, S. A. Douglas, and J. T. Stasko. A meta-study of algorithm visualization effectiveness. *Journal of Visual Languages & Computing*, 13(3):259–290, 2002. DOI: 10.1006/jvlc.2002.0237. 32

[150] R. M. Ingersoll. Teacher turnover and teacher shortages: an organizational analysis. *American Educational Research Journal*, 38(3):499–534, 2001. DOI: 10.3102/00028312038003499. 103

[151] C. Jackson. A little now for a lot later: A look at a Texas Advanced Placement incentive program. *Journal of Human Resources*, 45:591–639, 2010. DOI: 10.1353/jhr.2010.0019. 89

[152] M. C. Jadud. Methods and tools for exploring novice compilation behaviour. In *Proceedings of the Second International Workshop on Computing Education Research*, ICER '06, pages 73–84, New York, NY, USA, 2006. ACM. DOI: 10.1145/1151588.1151600. 79

[153] B. James DiSalvo, S. Yardi, M. Guzdial, T. McKlin, C. Meadows, K. Perry, and A. Bruckman. African American men constructing computing identity. In *CHI '11: Proceedings of the SIGCHI Conference on Human Factors in Computing Systems*, pages 2967–2970, New York, NY, USA, 2011. ACM. DOI: 10.1145/1978942.1979381. 88

[154] K. Jensen and N. Wirth. *PASCAL User Manual and Report*. Springer-Verlag New York, Inc., New York, NY, USA, 1974. 21

[155] W. L. Johnson and E. Soloway. Proust: Knowledge-based program understanding. In *Proceedings of the 7th International Conference on Software Engineering*, ICSE '84, pages 369–380, Piscataway, NJ, USA, 1984. IEEE Press. DOI: 10.1109/TSE.1985.232210. 22

[156] Joint Task Force on Computing Curricula, ACM/IEEE. Computer science curricula 2013. https://www.acm.org/education/CS2013-final-report.pdf, December 2013. 14

[157] S. P. Jones and S. Humphreys. Computing at school: A national working group. http://www.computingatschool.org.uk/data/uploads/Computing_at_School.pdf, August 2010. 4

[158] Y. B. Kafai. *Minds in play: Computer game design as a context for children's learning*. Routledge, 1995. 44

[159] Y. B. Kafai. Constructionism. In R. K. Sawyer, editor, *The Cambridge Handbook of the Learning Sciences*. Cambridge University Press, 2006. 27

[160] Y. B. Kafai and Q. Burke. *Connected Code: Why Children Need to Learn Programming*. MIT Press, Cambridge, MA, 2014. xvii

[161] Y. B. Kafai and C. C. Ching. Affordances of collaborative software design planning for elementary students' science talk. *Journal of the Learning Sciences*, 10(3):321–363, 2001. DOI: 10.1207/S15327809JLS1003_4. 44, 98

[162] Y. B. Kafai, D. A. Fields, and W. Q. Burke. Entering the clubhouse: Case studies of young programmers. *End-User Computing, Development, and Software Engineering: New Challenges: New Challenges*, page 279, 2012. DOI: 10.4018/joeuc.2010101906. 98

[163] Y. B. Kafai, E. Lee, K. Searle, D. Fields, E. Kaplan, and D. Lui. A crafts-oriented approach to computing in high school: Introducing computational concepts, practices, and perspectives with electronic textiles. *Transactions on Computing Education*, 14(1):1–20, 2014. DOI: 10.1145/2576874. 44

[164] Y. V. Kafai. Video game designs by girls and boys: variability and consistency of gender differences. In *From Barbie to Mortal Kombat: gender and computer games*, pages 90–114. MIT Press, Cambridge, MA, USA, 1998. 44

[165] D. Kahneman. *Thinking, fast and slow*. Macmillan, 2011. 62, 88, 104

[166] D. Kahneman, J. L. Knetsch, and R. H. Thaler. Anomalies: The endowment effect, loss aversion, and status quo bias. *The Journal of Economic Perspectives*, pages 193–206, 1991. DOI: 10.1257/jep.5.1.193. 84

[167] K. Karplus. Practice, teaching, or genetics. https://gasstationwithoutpumps.wordpress.com/2014/10/13/practice-teaching-or-genetics/, October 2013. 86

[168] A. Kay. Squeak etoys, children, and learning. http://www.squeakland.org/resources/articles/article.jsp?id=1009, August 2015. 99, 106

[169] A. Kay and A. Goldberg. Personal dynamic media. *IEEE Computer*, pages 31–41, 1977. DOI: 10.1109/C-M.1977.217672. xv, 1, 42, 107

[170] A. C. Kay. The early history of Smalltalk. In *The Second ACM SIGPLAN Conference on History of Programming Languages*, HOPL-II, pages 69–95, New York, NY, USA, 1993. ACM. DOI: 10.1145/154766.155364. 41, 107

[171] G. Keillor. The Lake Wobegon effect. http://www.publicradio.org/columns/prairiehome/posthost/2013/04/01/the_lake_wobegon_effect.php, April 2013. 15

[172] C. Kelleher and R. Pausch. Lowering the barriers to programming: A taxonomy of programming environments and languages for novice programmers. *ACM Computing Surveys*, 37(2):83–137, June 2005. DOI: 10.1145/1089733.1089734. 106

[173] D. Klahr and S. M. Carver. Cognitive objectives in a LOGO debugging curriculum: Instruction, learning, and transfer. *Cognitive Psychology*, 20(3):362–404, 1988. DOI: 10.1016/0010-0285(88)90004-7. 47

[174] M. Kleckler. State booting up computer-science courses. http://www.arkansasonline.com/news/2015/aug/02/state-booting-up-computer-science-cours/, 2015. 1

[175] H. Kohl. I won't learn from you. *Confronting student resistance in our classrooms. Teaching for Equity and Social Justice*, pages 134–135, 1994. 27

[176] J. L. Kolodner, J. Gray, and B. B. Fasse. Promoting transfer through case-based reasoning: Rituals and practices in learning by design classrooms. *Cognitive Science Quarterly*, 3(2):119–170, 2003. 29

[177] J. Krajcik, P. Blumenfeld, R. W. Marx, and E. Soloway. A collaborative model for helping science teachers learn project-based instruction. *Elementary School Journal*, 94(5):539–551, 1994. DOI: 10.1086/461782. 66

[178] S. Krishnamurthi. Programming in Pyret. http://www.pyret.org/, August 2015. 107

[179] D. M. Kurland, R. D. Pea, C. Clement, and R. Mawby. A study of the development of programming ability and thinking skills in high school students. *Journal of Educational Computing Research*, 2(4):429–458, 1986. DOI: 10.2190/BKML-B1QV-KDN4-8ULH. 46

[180] K. Lang, R. Galanos, J. Goode, D. Seehorn, and F. Trees. Bugs in the system: Computer science teacher certification in the US. Technical report, Computer Science Teachers Association (CSTA), 2013. 73, 74

[181] J. Larkin, J. McDemott, D. Simon, and H. Simon. Expert and novice performance in solving physics problems. *Science*, 208:140–156, 1980. DOI: 10.1126/science.208.4450.1335. 29, 31, 70

[182] J. Lave and E. Wenger. *Situated Learning: Legitimate Peripheral Participation*. Cambridge University Press, 1991. 13, 33

[183] C. B. Lee. Experience report: CS1 in MATLAB for non-majors, with Media Computation and Peer Instruction. In *Proceeding of the 44th ACM Technical Symposium on Computer Science Education*, SIGCSE '13, pages 35–40, New York, NY, USA, 2013. ACM. DOI: 10.1145/2445196.2445214. 64

[184] I. Lee, F. Martin, J. Denner, B. Coulter, W. Allan, J. Erickson, J. Malyn-Smith, and L. Werner. Computational thinking for youth in practice. *ACM Inroads*, 2(1):32–37, 2011. DOI: 10.1145/1929887.1929902. 49

[185] M. J. Lee, F. Bahmani, I. Kwan, J. LaFerte, P. Charters, A. Horvath, F. Luor, J. Cao, C. Law, M. Beswetherick, et al. Principles of a debugging-first puzzle game for computing education. In *Visual Languages and Human-Centric Computing (VL/HCC), 2014 IEEE Symposium on*, pages 57–64. IEEE, 2014. DOI: 10.1109/VLHCC.2014.6883023. 87

[186] M. J. Lee and A. J. Ko. Personifying programming tool feedback improves novice programmers' learning. In *Proceedings of the Seventh International Workshop on Computing Education Research*, ICER '11, pages 109–116, New York, NY, USA, 2011. ACM. DOI: 10.1145/2016911.2016934. 87, 94, 107

[187] M. J. Lee and A. J. Ko. Investigating the role of purposeful goals on novices' engagement in a programming game. In *Visual Languages and Human-Centric Computing (VL/HCC), 2012 IEEE Symposium on*, pages 163–166. IEEE, 2012. DOI: 10.1109/VLHCC.2012.6344507. 87

[188] M. J. Lee and A. J. Ko. Comparing the effectiveness of online learning approaches on cs1 learning outcomes. In *Proceedings of the Eleventh Annual International Conference on International Computing Education Research*, ICER '15, pages 237–246, New York, NY, USA, 2015. ACM. DOI: 10.1145/2787622.2787709. 87

[189] M. J. Lee, A. J. Ko, and I. Kwan. In-game assessments increase novice programmers' engagement and level completion speed. In *Proceedings of the ninth annual international ACM conference on International computing education research*, pages 153–160. ACM, 2013. DOI: 10.1145/2493394.2493410. 87

[190] S.-J. Leslie, A. Cimpian, M. Meyer, and E. Freeland. Expectations of brilliance underlie gender distributions across academic disciplines. *Science*, 347(6219):262–265, 2015. DOI: 10.1126/science.1261375. 85

[191] G. Lewandowski, D. J. Bouvier, R. McCartney, K. Sanders, and B. Simon. Commonsense computing (episode 3): Concurrency and concert tickets. In *Proceedings of the Third International Workshop on Computing Education Research*, ICER '07, pages 133–144, New York, NY, USA, 2007. ACM. DOI: 10.1145/1288580.1288598. 85

[192] C. Lewis, M. H. Jackson, and W. M. Waite. Student and faculty attitudes and beliefs about computer science. *Communications of the ACM*, 53(5):78–85, May 2010. DOI: 10.1145/1735223.1735244. 84

[193] C. M. Lewis, K. Yasuhara, and R. E. Anderson. Deciding to major in computer science: A grounded theory of students' self-assessment of ability. In *Proceedings of the Seventh International Workshop on Computing Education Research*, ICER '11, pages 3–10, New York, NY, USA, 2011. ACM. DOI: 10.1145/2016911.2016915. 84

[194] R. Lister. Geek genes and bimodal grades. *ACM Inroads*, 1(3):16–17, Sept. 2011. DOI: 10.1145/2003616.2003622. 85

[195] R. Lister. Teaching-oriented faculty and computing education research. *ACM Inroads*, 3(1):22–23, Mar. 2012. DOI: 10.1145/2077808.2077814. 105

[196] R. Lister, E. S. Adams, S. Fitzgerald, W. Fone, J. Hamer, M. Lindholm, R. McCartney, J. E. Moström, K. Sanders, O. Seppälä, B. Simon, and L. Thomas. A multi-national study of reading and tracing skills in novice programmers. *SIGCSE Bulletin*, 36:119–150, June 2004. DOI: 10.1145/1041624.1041673. 3, 14, 23

[197] D. C. Littman, J. Pinto, S. Letovsky, and E. Soloway. Mental models and software maintenance. In *Papers presented at the first workshop on empirical studies of programmers on Empirical studies of programmers*, pages 80–98, Norwood, NJ, USA, 1986. Ablex Publishing Corp. DOI: 10.1016/0164-1212(87)90033-1. 31

[198] K. Luchini, C. Quintana, and E. Soloway. Pocket PiCoMap: a case study in designing and assessing a handheld concept mapping tool for learners. In *CHI '03: Proceedings of the SIGCHI Conference on Human Factors in Computing Systems*, pages 321–328, New York, NY, USA, 2003. ACM. DOI: 10.1145/642611.642668. 69

[199] K. Luchini, C. Quintana, and E. Soloway. Design guidelines for learner-centered hand-held tools. In *CHI '04: Proceedings of the SIGCHI Conference on Human Factors in Computing Systems*, pages 135–142, New York, NY, USA, 2004. ACM. DOI: 10.1145/985692.985710. 69

[200] A. L. Luehmann. Identity development as a lens to science teacher preparation. *Science Education*, 9(5):822–839, 2007. DOI: 10.1002/sce.20209. 76

[201] J. Maloney, M. Resnick, N. Rusk, B. Silverman, and E. Eastmond. The Scratch programming language and environment. *Transactions on Computing Education*, 10(4):16:1–16:15, Nov. 2010. DOI: 10.1145/1868358.1868363. 101, 106

[202] J. H. Maloney, K. Peppler, Y. Kafai, M. Resnick, and N. Rusk. Programming by choice: urban youth learning programming with Scratch. In *SIGCSE '08: Proceedings of the 39th SIGCSE technical symposium on computer science education*, pages 367–371. ACM, 2008. DOI: 10.1145/1352135.1352260. 106

[203] J. Margolis, R. Estrella, J. Goode, J. J. Holme, and K. Nao. *Stuck in the Shallow End: Education, Race, and Computing*. MIT Press, Cambridge, MA, 2008. xvii, 10, 84, 87

[204] J. Margolis and A. Fisher. *Unlocking the Clubhouse: Women in Computing*. MIT Press, 2002. 10, 55, 56, 83, 84, 87, 93

[205] L. E. Margulieux, R. Catrambone, and M. Guzdial. Subgoal labeled worked examples improve K-12 teacher performance in computer programming training. In M. Knauff, M. Pauen, N. Sebanz, and I. Wachsmuth, editors, *Proceedings of the 35th Annual Conference of the Cognitive Science Society*, pages 978–983. Cognitive Science Society, 2013. 79, 87

[206] L. E. Margulieux, M. Guzdial, and R. Catrambone. Subgoal-labeled instructional material improves performance and transfer in learning to develop mobile applications. In *Proceedings of the Ninth Annual International Conference on International Computing Education Research*, ICER '12, pages 71–78, New York, NY, USA, 2012. ACM. DOI: 10.1145/2361276.2361291. 79

[207] M. McCracken, V. Almstrum, D. Diaz, M. Guzdial, D. Hagan, Y. B.-D. Kolikant, C. Laxer, L. Thomas, I. Utting, and T. Wilusz. A multi-national, multi-institutional study of assessment of programming skills of first-year CS students. *ACM SIGCSE Bulletin*, 33(4):125–140, 2001. DOI: 10.1145/572139.572181. 23

[208] D. S. McCrickard and C. Lewis. Designing for cognitive limitations. In *Proceedings of the Designing Interactive Systems Conference*, DIS '12, pages 805–806, New York, NY, USA, 2012. ACM. DOI: 10.1145/2317956.2318083. 15

[209] C. McDowell, L. Werner, H. Bullock, and J. Fernald. The effects of pair-programming on performance in an introductory programming course. In *ACM SIGCSE Bulletin*, volume 34, pages 38–42. ACM, 2002. DOI: 10.1145/563517.563353. 87

[210] C. McDowell, L. Werner, H. E. Bullock, and J. Fernald. Pair programming improves student retention, confidence, and program quality. *Communications of the ACM*, 49(8):90–95, 2006. DOI: 10.1145/1145287.1145293. 87

[211] J. McGregor. Google's diversity numbers changed little in past year. http://www.washingtonpost.com/news/on-leadership/wp/2015/06/01/googles-diversity-numbers-changed-little-in-past-year/, June 2015. 8, 97

[212] M. H. McLuhan. *The Gutenberg Galaxy: The Making of Typographic Man*. University of Toronto Press, 1962. 5

[213] M. H. McLuhan. *Understanding Media: The Extensions of Man*. MIT Press, Cambridge, MA, 1964. 6

[214] E. Mechaber. President Obama is the first president to write a line of code. https://www.whitehouse.gov/blog/2014/12/10/president-obama-first-president-write-line-code, August 2015. 1

[215] B. N. Miller and D. L. Ranum. *Python programming in context*. Jones & Bartlett Publishers, 2014. 64

[216] J. Miller. Teacher's vision, but done New York City's way. *New York Times*, March 2013. 13

[217] L. A. Miller. Natural language programming: Styles, strategies, and contrasts. *IBM Systems Journal*, 20(2):184–215, 1981. DOI: 10.1147/sj.202.0184. 59

[218] B. B. Morrison, L. E. Margulieux, and M. Guzdial. Subgoals, context, and worked examples in learning computing problem solving. In *Proceedings of the Eleventh Annual International Conference on International Computing Education Research*, ICER '15, pages 21–29, New York, NY, USA, 2015. ACM. DOI: 10.1145/2787622.2787733. 29, 79, 87

[219] B. B. Morrison, L. Ni, and M. Guzdial. Adapting the disciplinary commons model for high school teachers: improving recruitment, creating community. In *Proceedings of the ninth annual international conference on International computing education research*, ICER '12, pages 47–54, New York, NY, USA, 2012. ACM. DOI: 10.1145/2361276.2361287. 77

[220] B. A. Nardi. *A small matter of programming: perspectives on end user computing*. MIT press, 1993. 69, 90

[221] M. J. Nathan, K. R. Koedinger, and M. Alibali. Expert blind spot: When content knowledge eclipses pedagogical content knowledge. In L. Chen, editor, *Proceedings of the Third International Conference on Cognitive Science*, pages 644–648. University of Science and Technology of China Press, 2001. 29, 33, 59, 106

[222] J. Naughton. Why all our kids should be taught how to code. http://www.theguardian.com/education/2012/mar/31/why-kids-should-be-taught-code, March 2012. 5

[223] N. S. Newcombe. Picture this: Increasing math and science learning by improving spatial thinking. *American Educator*, pages 29–43, 2010. 86

[224] A. Newell, A. J. Perlis, and H. A. Simon. Computer science. *Science*, 157(3795):1373–1374, 1967. DOI: 10.1126/science.157.3795.1373-b. 4

[225] L. Ni. *Building professional identity as computer science teachers: Supporting high school computer science teachers through reflection and community building.* Ph.D. thesis, Georgia Institute of Technology, Atlanta, GA, December 2011. 75, 76, 77, 102

[226] L. Ni and M. Guzdial. Prepare and support computer science (CS) teachers: Understanding CS teachers' professional identity, 2011. 76

[227] L. Ni, M. Guzdial, A. E. Tew, B. Morrison, and R. Galanos. Building a community to support HS CS teachers: the disciplinary commons for computing educators. In *SIGCSE '11: Proceedings of the 42nd ACM technical symposium on Computer science education*, pages 553–558, New York, NY, USA, 2011. ACM. DOI: 10.1145/1953163.1953319. 77

[228] L. Ni, T. McKlin, and M. Guzdial. How do computing faculty adopt curriculum innovations?: The story from instructors. In *Proceedings of the 41st ACM Technical Symposium on Computer Science Education*, SIGCSE '10, pages 544–548, New York, NY, USA, 2010. ACM. DOI: 10.1145/1734263.1734444. 77, 87

[229] T. J. Nokes. Mechanisms of knowledge transfer. *Thinking and Reasoning*, 15(1):1–36, 2009. DOI: 10.1080/13546780802490186. 28

[230] D. Norman. *The design of everyday things.* Basic Books, New York, NY, 2002. 15

[231] R. Noss and C. Hoyles. *Windows on mathematical meanings: Learning cultures and computers*, volume 17. Springer Science & Business Media, 1996. DOI: 10.1007/978-94-009-1696-8. 47

[232] OECD Education Committee. *Teachers Matter: Attracting, Developing and Retaining Effective Teachers.* OECD, 2005. 85

[233] G. M. Olson, R. Catrambone, and E. Soloway. *Programming and algebra word problems: a failure to transfer*, pages 1–13. Ablex Publishing Corp., Norwood, NJ, USA, 1987. 30

[234] N. R. Orit Hazzan, Tami Lapidot. *Guide to Teaching Computer Science: An Activity-Based Approach*. Springer, 2011. xv

[235] D. B. Palumbo. Programming language/problem-solving research: A review of relevant issues. *Review of Educational Research*, 60(1):65–89, 1990. DOI: 10.3102/00346543060001065. 47

[236] J. F. Pane, B. A. Myers, and C. A. Ratanamahatana. Studying the language and structure in non-programmers' solutions to programming problems. *International Journal of Human-Computer Studies*, 54(2):237–264, 2001. DOI: 10.1006/ijhc.2000.0410. 50, 59

[237] S. Papert. Teaching children to be mathematicians versus teaching about mathematics. Technical report, MIT AI Laboratory, 1971. 41

[238] S. Papert. *Mindstorms: Children, computers, and powerful ideas*. Basic Books, 1980. 1, 41

[239] S. Papert. Situating constructionism. In I. Harel and S. Papert, editors, *Constructionism*, pages 1–11. Ablex Publishing Company, 1991. 41

[240] T. H. Park, B. Dorn, and A. Forte. An analysis of HTML and CSS syntax errors in a web development course. *Transactions on Computing Education*, 15(1):1–21, 2015. DOI: 10.1145/2700514. 70

[241] T. H. Park, A. Saxena, S. Jagannath, S. Wiedenbeck, and A. Forte. Towards a taxonomy of errors in HTML and CSS. In *ICER '13: Proceedings of the ninth annual international ACM conference on International computing education research*, pages 75–82, New York, NY, USA, 2013. ACM. DOI: 10.1145/2493394.2493405. 70

[242] D. Parsons and P. Haden. Parson's programming puzzles: A fun and effective learning tool for first programming courses. In *Proceedings of the 8th Australasian Conference on Computing Education - Volume 52*, ACE '06, pages 157–163, Darlinghurst, Australia, Australia, 2006. Australian Computer Society, Inc. 79

[243] A. M. Paul. Are college lectures unfair? *New York Times*, September 12 2015. 106

[244] R. D. Pea. Language-independent conceptual "bugs" in novice programming. *Journal of Educational Computing Research*, 1(1986), 2. 30, 50

[245] R. D. Pea and D. M. Kurland. On the cognitive effects of learning computer programming. *New Ideas in Psychology*, 2:137–168, 1984. DOI: 10.1016/0732-118X(84)90018-7. 46

[246] R. D. Pea, D. M. Kurland, and J. Hawkins. Logo programming and the development of thinking skills. In M. Chen and W. Paisley, editors, *Children and microcomputers: Formative studies*. Sage, Beverly Hills, CA, 1985. 46

[247] K. A. Peppler and Y. B. Kafai. Youth as media art designers: workshops for creative coding. In *IDC '08: Proceedings of the 7th international conference on Interaction design and children*, pages 137–140, New York, NY, USA, 2008. ACM. DOI: 10.1145/1463689.1463740. 44

[248] K. Petram. Bloom's taxonomy: Levels of understanding. http://www.psia-nw.org/new sletter-articles/blooms-taxonomy-levels-of-understanding/, June 2010. 12

[249] J. Piaget, M. Cook, and W. Norton. *The origins of intelligence in children*. International Universities Press New York, 1952. 98

[250] E. S. Poole. Interacting with infrastructure: A case for breaching experiments in home computing research. In *Proceedings of the ACM 2012 Conference on Computer Supported Cooperative Work*, CSCW '12, pages 759–768, New York, NY, USA, 2012. ACM. DOI: 10.1145/2145204.2145319. 7

[251] L. Porter, C. Bailey Lee, and B. Simon. Halving fail rates using peer instruction: a study of four computer science courses. In *Proceeding of the 44th ACM technical symposium on Computer science education*, pages 177–182. ACM, 2013. DOI: 10.1145/2445196.2445250. 87

[252] L. Porter, C. Bailey Lee, B. Simon, Q. Cutts, and D. Zingaro. Experience report: a multi-classroom report on the value of peer instruction. In *Proceedings of the 16th annual joint conference on Innovation and technology in computer science education*, pages 138–142. ACM, 2011. DOI: 10.1145/1999747.1999788. 87

[253] L. Porter, M. Guzdial, C. McDowell, and B. Simon. Success in introductory programming: What works? *Communications of the ACM*, 56(8):34–36, Aug. 2013. DOI: 10.1145/2492007.2492020. 64, 87

[254] L. Porter and B. Simon. Retaining nearly one-third more majors with a trio of instructional best practices in CS1. In *Proceeding of the 44th ACM Technical Symposium on Computer Science Education*, SIGCSE '13, pages 165–170, New York, NY, USA, 2013. ACM. DOI: 10.1145/2445196.2445248. 64, 87

[255] L. Porter, D. Zingaro, and R. Lister. Predicting student success using fine grain clicker data. In *Proceedings of the Tenth Annual Conference on International Computing Education Research*, ICER '14, pages 51–58, New York, NY, USA, 2014. ACM. DOI: 10.1145/2632320.2632354. 86

[256] E. Post. Real programmers don't use PASCAL. http://www.webcitation.org/659y h1oSh, July 1983. 89

[257] C. Quintana, K. Abotel, and E. Soloway. NoRIS: Supporting computational science activities through learner-centered design. In *Proceedings of the 1996 International Conference on*

Learning Sciences, ICLS '96, pages 272–279. International Society of the Learning Sciences, 1996. 69

[258] C. Quintana, E. Soloway, and J. Krajcik. Issues and approaches for developing learner-centered technology. In M. Zelkowitz, editor, *Advances in Computers*, volume 57, pages 271–321. Academic Press Ltd., New York, NY, USA, 2003. 69

[259] S. A. Rebelsky, J. Davis, and J. Weinman. Building knowledge and confidence with Mediascripting: A successful interdisciplinary approach to CS1. In *Proceeding of the 44th ACM Technical Symposium on Computer Science Education*, SIGCSE '13, pages 483–488, New York, NY, USA, 2013. ACM. DOI: 10.1145/2445196.2445342. 64

[260] M. Resnick. Multilogo: A study of children and concurrent programming. *Interactive Learning Environments*, 1(3):153–170, 1990. DOI: 10.1080/104948290010301. 32

[261] M. Resnick. Starlogo: an environment for decentralized modeling and decentralized thinking. In *CHI '96: Conference Companion on Human Factors in Computing Systems*, pages 11–12, New York, NY, USA, 1996. ACM. DOI: 10.1145/257089.257095. 99

[262] M. Resnick and D. Siegel. A different approach to coding. `https://medium.com/bright/a-different-approach-to-coding-d679b06d83a`, November 2015. 6, 96

[263] L. Rich, H. Perry, and M. Guzdial. A CS1 course designed to address interests of women. In *Proceedings of the ACM SIGCSE Conference*, pages 190–194, 2004. DOI: 10.1145/971300.971370. 55, 62

[264] E. Roberts. Computing Curricula 2001. *Journal of Educational Resources in Computing*, 1(3es), Sept. 2001. 56, 66

[265] E. Roberts, C. F. Cover, G. Davies, M. Schneider, and R. Sloan. Computing Curricula 2001: Implementing the recommendations. In *Proceedings of the 33rd SIGCSE Technical Symposium on Computer Science Education*, SIGCSE '02, pages 167–168, New York, NY, USA, 2002. ACM. DOI: 10.1145/563340.563403. 56, 66

[266] A. Robins. Learning edge momentum: A new account of outcomes in CS1. *Computer Science Education*, 20(1):37–71, 2010. DOI: 10.1080/08993401003612167. 87

[267] J. Rode, M. B. Rosson, M. A. P.-Q. Qui, et al. End user development of web applications. In *End User Development*, pages 161–182. Springer, 2006. DOI: 10.1007/1-4020-5386-X_8. 70

[268] S. H. Rodger. Introduction to program design. `https://www.cs.duke.edu/courses/spring01/cps049s/assign/las_chapter1.pdf`, January 2001. 85

[269] B. Ross. Remindings and their effects in learning a cognitive skill. *Cognitive Psychology*, 16:371–416, 1980. DOI: 10.1016/0010-0285(84)90014-8. 28

[270] B. H. Ross. This is like that: The use of earlier problems and the separation of similarity effects. *Journal of Experimental Psychology: Learning, Memory, and Cognition*, 13(629–639), 1987. DOI: 10.1037/0278-7393.13.4.629. 28

[271] M. B. Rosson, J. Ballin, and J. Rode. Who, what, and how: A survey of informal and professional web developers. In *Visual Languages and Human-Centric Computing, 2005 IEEE Symposium on*, pages 199–206. IEEE, 2005. DOI: 10.1109/VLHCC.2005.73. 70

[272] P. M. Sadler, G. Sonnert, H. P. Coyle, N. Cook-Smith, and J. L. Miller. The influence of teachers' knowledge on student learning in middle school physical science classrooms. *American Educational Research Journal*, 50(5):1020–1049, 2013. DOI: 10.3102/0002831213477680. 33

[273] R. K. Sawyer, A. Collins, J. Confrey, J. L. Kolodner, and M. Scardamalia. Moving forward: The learning sciences and the future of education. In *Proceedings of the 7th International Conference on Learning Sciences*, ICLS '06, pages 1084–1087. International Society of the Learning Sciences, 2006. 29

[274] C. Scaffidi, M. Shaw, and B. Myers. An approach for categorizing end user programmers to guide software engineering research. *SIGSOFT Software Engineering Notes*, 30(4):1–5, May 2005. DOI: 10.1145/1082983.1083096. 6, 68, 90, 104

[275] M. Scardamalia and C. Bereiter. Knowledge telling and knowledge transforming in written composition. *Advances in Applied Psycholinguistics*, 2:142–175, 1987. 7, 96

[276] E. Schanzer, K. Fisler, S. Krishnamurthi, and M. Felleisen. Transferring skills at solving word problems from computing to algebra through Bootstrap. In *Proceedings of the 46th ACM Technical Symposium on Computer Science Education*, SIGCSE '15, pages 616–621, New York, NY, USA, 2015. ACM. DOI: 10.1145/2676723.2677238. 6, 49

[277] D. L. Schwartz and J. D. Bransford. A time for telling. *Cognition and Instruction*, 16:475–522, 1998. DOI: 10.1207/s1532690xci1604_4. 29

[278] D. L. Schwartz and T. Martin. Inventing to prepare for future learning: The hidden efficiency of encouraging original student production in statistics instruction. *Cognition and Instruction*, 22(2):129–184, 2004. DOI: 10.1207/s1532690xci2202_1. 50, 98

[279] K. A. Searle and Y. B. Kafai. Boys' needlework: Understanding gendered and indigenous perspectives on computing and crafting with electronic textiles. In *ICER '15: Proceedings of the eleventh annual International Conference on International Computing Education Research*, pages 31–39, New York, NY, USA, 2015. ACM. DOI: 10.1145/2787622.2787724. 44

[280] R. L. Shackelford. *Introduction to Computing and Algorithms*. Addison-Wesley Longman Publishing Co., Inc., Boston, MA, USA, 1st edition, 1997. 53

[281] D. W. Shaffer and M. Resnick. "Thick" authenticity: new media and authentic learning. *Journal of Interactive Learning Research*, 10(2):195–215, 1999. 4, 14, 61

[282] B. L. Sherin. A comparison of programming languages and algebraic notation as expressive langauges for physics. *International Journal of Computers for Mathematical Learning*, 6:1–61, 2001. DOI: 10.1023/A:1011434026437. 31, 43, 45, 49, 50

[283] B. Shneiderman. Exploratory experiments in programmer behavior. *International Journal of Computing and Information Science*, 5(2):123–143, 1976. DOI: 10.1007/BF00975629. 29

[284] C. Simard, A. D. Henderson, S. K. Gilmartin, L. Schiebinger, and T. Whitney. Climbing the technical ladder: Obstacles and solutions for mid-level women in technology. http://anitaborg.org/wp-content/uploads/2013/12/Climbing_the_Technical_Ladder.pdf, 2004. 79

[285] S. Simmons, B. DiSalvo, and M. Guzdial. Using game development to reveal programming competency. In *FDG '12: Proceedings of the International Conference on the Foundations of Digital Games*, pages 89–96, New York, NY, USA, 2012. ACM. DOI: 10.1145/2282338.2282359. 88

[286] B. Simon, T.-Y. Chen, G. Lewandowski, R. McCartney, and K. Sanders. Commonsense computing: What students know before we teach (episode 1: Sorting). In *Proceedings of the Second International Workshop on Computing Education Research*, ICER '06, pages 29–40, New York, NY, USA, 2006. ACM. DOI: 10.1145/1151588.1151594. 85

[287] B. Simon and Q. Cutts. Peer instruction: A teaching method to foster deep understanding. *Communications of the ACM*, 55(2):27–29, 2012. DOI: 10.1145/2076450.2076459. 87

[288] B. Simon, P. Kinnunen, L. Porter, and D. Zazkis. Experience report: CS1 for majors with media computation. In *Proceedings of the fifteenth annual conference on Innovation and technology in computer science education*, ITiCSE '10, pages 214–218, New York, NY, USA, 2010. ACM. DOI: 10.1145/1822090.1822151. 64

[289] R. H. Sloan and P. Troy. CS 0.5: a better approach to introductory computer science for majors. *ACM SIGCSE Bulletin*, 40:271–275, 2008. DOI: 10.1145/1352322.1352230. 64

[290] D. M. Smith. *Engineering computation with MATLAB*. Pearson/Addison Wesley, 2008. 55, 56

[291] C. Snow. *The Two Cultures*. Cambridge University Press, London, 1959. 39

[292] C. Solomon. *Computer environments for children: A reflection on theories of learning and education*. The MIT Press, Cambridge, Mass., 1986. 1

[293] E. Soloway, J. Bonar, and K. Ehrlich. Cognitive strategies and looping constructs: An empirical study. *Communications of the ACM*, 26(11):853–860, Nov. 1983. DOI: 10.1145/182.358436. 22

[294] E. Soloway, K. Ehrlich, and J. Bonar. Tapping into tacit programming knowledge. In *Proceedings of the 1982 Conference on Human Factors in Computing Systems*, CHI '82, pages 52–57, New York, NY, USA, 1982. ACM. DOI: 10.1145/800049.801754. 21

[295] E. Soloway, M. Guzdial, and K. E. Hay. Learner-centered design: The challenge for hci in the 21st century. *Interactions*, 1(2):36–48, 1994. DOI: 10.1145/174809.174813. 15, 44

[296] E. Soloway, S. L. Jackson, J. Klein, C. Quintana, J. Reed, J. Spitulnik, S. J. Stratford, S. Studer, J. Eng, and N. Scala. Learning theory in practice: Case studies of learner-centered design. In *Proceedings of the SIGCHI Conference on Human Factors in Computing Systems*, CHI '96, pages 189–196, New York, NY, USA, 1996. ACM. DOI: 10.1145/238386.238476. 69

[297] J. Sorva. *Visual Program Simulation in Introductory Programming Education*. Doctor of science in technology, Aalto University School of Science, 2012. 32, 50

[298] J. Sorva. Notional machines and introductory programming education. *Transactions on Computing Education*, 13(2):8:1–8:31, July 2013. DOI: 10.1145/2490822. 31

[299] J. Sorva, V. Karavirta, and L. Malmi. A review of generic program visualization systems for introductory programming education. *Transactions on Computing Education*, 13(4):15:1–15:64, Nov. 2013. DOI: 10.1145/2483710.2483713. 32

[300] J. C. Spohrer. *Marcel: Simulating the novice programmer*. Ablex, Norwood, NJ, 1992. 22

[301] StackOverflow. What is a "real" programming language? http://stackoverflow.com/questions/3222316/what-is-a-real-programming-language, February 2012. 89

[302] A. Stefik and S. Siebert. An empirical investigation into programming language syntax. *Transactions on Computing Education*, 13(4):19:1–19:40, Nov. 2013. DOI: 10.1145/2534973. 107

[303] L. A. Stein. Interaction, computation, and education. In D. Goldin, S. A. Smolka, and P. Wegner, editors, *Interactive Computation: The New Paradigm*. Springer, 2006. 85

[304] R. Stevens, K. O'Connor, L. Garrison, A. Jocuns, and D. M. Amos. Becoming an engineer: Toward a three dimensional view of engineering learning. *Journal of Engineering Education*, 97(3):355–368, 2008. DOI: 10.1002/j.2168-9830.2008.tb00984.x. 14, 62

[305] J. Summet, D. Kumar, K. O'Hara, D. Walker, L. Ni, D. Blank, and T. Balch. Personalizing CS1 with robots. In *Proceedings of the 40th ACM Technical Symposium on Computer Science Education*, SIGCSE '09, pages 433–437, New York, NY, USA, 2009. ACM. DOI: 10.1145/1508865.1509018. 64

[306] J. Sweller. Cognitive load during problem solving: Effects on learning. *Cognitive Science*, 12:257–285, 1988. Theory behind worked examples. DOI: 10.1207/s15516709cog1202_4. 87

[307] R. Taub, M. Armoni, and M. Ben-Ari. CS Unplugged and middle-school students’ views, attitudes, and intentions regarding CS. *Transactions on Computing Education*, 12(2):8:1–8:29, Apr. 2012. DOI: 10.1145/2160547.2160551. 40

[308] K. Taylor and C. C. Miller. De Blasio to announce 10-year deadline to offer computer science to all students. http://www.nytimes.com/2015/09/16/nyregion/de-blasio-to-announce-10-year-deadline-to-offer-computer-science-to-all-students.html?_r=0, 2015. 1

[309] D. Teague and R. Lister. Programming: reading, writing and reversing. In *ITiCSE '14: Proceedings of the 2014 conference on Innovation & technology in computer science education*, pages 285–290, New York, NY, USA, 2014. ACM. DOI: 10.1145/2591708.2591712. 3, 14

[310] J. Tenenberg and S. Fincher. Opening the door of the computer science classroom: the disciplinary commons. In *SIGCSE '07: Proceedings of the 38th SIGCSE technical symposium on Computer science education*, pages 514–518, New York, NY, USA, 2007. ACM. DOI: 10.1145/1227310.1227484. 77

[311] M. S. Terlecki, N. S. Newcombe, and M. Little. Durable and generalized effects of spatial experience on mental rotation: Gender differences in growth patterns. *Applied Cognitive Psychology*, 22(7):996–1013, 2008. DOI: 10.1002/acp.1420. 86

[312] A. E. Tew. *Assessing fundamental introductory computing concept knowledge in a language independent manner*. Ph.D. thesis, College of Computing, Georgia Institute of Technology, 2010. 26

[313] A. E. Tew, B. Dorn, J. William D. Leahy, and M. Guzdial. Context as support for learning computer organization. *Journal of Education Resources in Computing*, 8(3):1–18, 2008. DOI: 10.1145/1404935.1404937. 92

[314] A. E. Tew, C. Fowler, and M. Guzdial. Tracking an innovation in introductory CS education from a research university to a two-year college. In *SIGCSE '05: Proceedings of the 36th SIGCSE technical symposium on Computer science education*, pages 416–420, New York, NY, USA, 2005. ACM. DOI: 10.1145/1047344.1047481. 62, 64, 66

[315] A. E. Tew and M. Guzdial. Developing a validated assessment of fundamental CS1 concepts. In *Proceedings of the 41st ACM technical symposium on Computer science education*, SIGCSE '10, pages 97–101, New York, NY, USA, 2010. ACM. DOI: 10.1145/1734263.1734297. 26

[316] A. E. Tew and M. Guzdial. The FCS1: a language independent assessment of CS1 knowledge. In *SIGCSE '11: Proceedings of the 42nd ACM technical symposium on Computer science education*, pages 111–116, New York, NY, USA, 2011. ACM. DOI: 10.1145/1953163.1953200. 26

[317] A. E. Tew, M. McCracken, and M. Guzdial. Impact of alternative introductory courses on programming concept understanding. In *Proceedings of the first International Computing Education Research Workshop*, New York, NY, 2005. ACM SIGCSE, ACM. DOI: 10.1145/1089786.1089789. 24

[318] J. G. Trafton and B. J. Reiser. *The contributions of studying examples and solving problems to skill acquisition*, pages 1017–1022. Lawrence Erlbaum Associates, Inc., Hillsdale, NJ, 1993. 79

[319] I. Utting, A. E. Tew, M. McCracken, L. Thomas, D. Bouvier, R. Frye, J. Paterson, M. Caspersen, Y. B.-D. Kolikant, J. Sorva, and T. Wilusz. A fresh look at novice programmers' performance and their teachers' expectations. In *Proceedings of the ITiCSE Working Group Reports Conference on Innovation and Technology in Computer Science Education-working Group Reports*, ITiCSE -WGR '13, pages 15–32, New York, NY, USA, 2013. ACM. DOI: 10.1145/2543882.2543884. 24

[320] A. Wigfield and J. S. Eccles. Expectancy–value theory of achievement motivation. *Contemporary Educational Psychology*, 25(1):68–81, 2000. DOI: 10.1006/ceps.1999.1015. 34, 35

[321] Wikipedia. Grounded theory. https://en.wikipedia.org/wiki/Grounded_theory, March 2015. 91

[322] Wikipedia. Inert knowledge. https://en.wikipedia.org/wiki/Inert_knowledge, August 2015. 28

[323] U. Wilensky, C. E. Brady, and M. S. Horn. Fostering computational literacy in science classrooms. *Communications of the ACM*, 57(8):24–28, Aug. 2014. DOI: 10.1145/2633031. 49, 99

[324] G. Wilson. Software carpentry. https://software-carpentry.org/, August 2015. 68

[325] J. Wing. Computational thinking: What and why. *The Link*, 2010. 4

[326] J. M. Wing. Computational thinking. *Communications of the ACM*, 49(3):33–35, Mar. 2006. DOI: 10.1145/1118178.1118215. 4, 40

[327] D. Wood, J. S. Bruner, and G. Ross. The role of tutoring in problem-solving. *Journal of Child Psychology and Psychiatry*, 17:89–100, 1975. DOI: 10.1111/j.1469-7610.1976.tb00381.x. 44

[328] R. Wright, W. L. Thompson, G. Ganis, N. S. Newcombe, and S. M. Kosslyn. Training generalized spatial skills. *Psychonomic Bulletin & Review*, 15(4):763–771, 2008. DOI: 10.3758/PBR.15.4.763. 86

[329] S. Yardi and A. Bruckman. What is computing?: bridging the gap between teenagers' perceptions and graduate students' experiences. In *Proceedings of the third international workshop on Computing education research*, pages 39–50. ACM, 2007. DOI: 10.1145/1288580.1288586. 56

[330] S. Yarosh and M. Guzdial. Narrating data structures: The role of context in CS2. *Journal of Educational Resources in Computing*, 7(4):Article 6, 2008. DOI: 10.1145/1316450.1316456. 66

[331] P. Yongpradit. What are Code.org's costs per teach, cost per student? https://code.org/about/evaluation/costs, 2015 June. 103

[332] D. Yoo, E. Schanzer, S. Krishnamurthi, and K. Fisler. WeScheme: The browser is your programming environment. In *Proceedings of the 16th Annual Joint Conference on Innovation and Technology in Computer Science Education*, ITiCSE '11, pages 163–167, New York, NY, USA, 2011. ACM. DOI: 10.1145/1999747.1999795. 49

[333] N. Young. Computatational thinking. http://greenlightgo.org/education/courses/engr101fall2014/2014/12/02/computational-thinking-tuth1100-nicolas-young-2/, December 2014. 85

Author's Biography

MARK GUZDIAL

Mark Guzdial is a Professor in the College of Computing at Georgia Institute of Technology. Mark is a member of the GVU Center. He received his Ph.D. in education and computer science (a joint degree) at the University of Michigan in 1993, where he developed Emile, an environment for high school science learners programming multimedia demonstrations and physics simulations. He was the original developer of the CoWeb (or Swiki), which has been a widely used Wiki engine in universities around the world. He is the inventor of the Media Computation approach to learning introductory computing, which uses contextualized computing education to attract and retain students. He was vice-chair of the ACM Education Board, and still serves on the ACM Education Council. He serves on the editorial boards of *ACM Transactions on Computing Education* and *Journal of the Learning Sciences*. His blog on computing education is active, with over 500 pageviews per day. He and his wife were awarded the 2010 ACM Karl V. Karlstrom Outstanding Educator Award, he was awarded the IEEE Computer Society Undergraduate Teaching Award in 2012, and in 2014, he was named an ACM Distinguished Educator and a Fellow of the ACM.

Index